More Write Dance

A Lucky Duck Book

More Write Dance

Ragnhild A Oussoren

P·C·P

Paul Chapman
Publishing

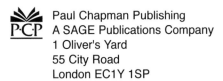 Paul Chapman Publishing
A SAGE Publications Company
1 Oliver's Yard
55 City Road
London EC1Y 1SP

SAGE Publications Inc.
2455 Teller Road
Thousand Oaks, California 91320

SAGE Publications India Pvt Ltd
B 1/I 1 Mohan Cooperative Industrial Area
Mathura Road
New Delhi 110 044

SAGE Publications Asia-Pacific Pte Ltd
33 Pekin Street #02-01
Far East Square
Singapore 048763

A catalogue record for this book is available from the British Library

ISBN 978 1 4129 2264 7
ISBN 978 1 4129 1871 8 (pbk)

Library of Congress Control Number 2006940661

Commissioning editors: George Robinson, Barbara Maines
Editorial team: Mel Maines, Sarah Lynch, Wendy Ogden
Designer: Helen Weller
Illustrator: Ragnhild A Oussoren

Printed on paper from sustainable resources
Printed in Great Britain by Cromwell Press Ltd, Trowbridge, Wiltshire

Contents

Important

This programme consists of this book, a music CD, a resources CD and a DVD of footage designed to complement the text. This book is the main part of the programme.

The DVD

This was filmed in Dutch schools and has no 'voice-over' or spoken soundtrack. There are eight sections and each should be watched after reading the appropriate chapter in the book. The DVD was not intended to be watched in one sitting; reading the book is essential and the visual images on the DVD support and help to clarify the text.

The eight sections

1. Write Drawing (Chapter 2)
2. Learning to Write (Chapter 3)
3-8. Music Drawings (Chapter 4)
        Sailing Boat
        Ocean Journey
        Little Tea Ship
        Dream Castle
        Star Home
        Snow

The music CD

There are 29 tracks that are arranged in the six themes of the Music Drawings. The index indicates the theme, the part of theme, whether the music stimulates rhythm for round or straight movement and the running time.

Throughout the book, track numbers are provided for the various exercises and tracks are also indicated for the original Write Dance and Write Dance in the Nursery. These are useful extra music resources but are not essential.

Track	Title	Part	Straight/round	Speed	Time
1	Sailing Boat		Straight/round	Moderate	3:02
2	Ocean Journey	Night	Round	Slow	1:11
3		Morning	Round	Slow	0:48
4		Fishing boat	Round	Slow	2:06
5		Whirlwinds	Round	Slow	0:35
6		Island	Round	Slow	1:37
7		Party	Straight/Round	Fast	2:07
8	Little Tea Ship		Round	Moderate	1:36
9	Dream Castle	Stepped Gable	Straight	Moderate	0:51
10		Roofs and Climbing Roses	Straight/Round	Moderate	3:09
11		Bouncing Ball	Round	Fast	1:06
12		Brickwork	Straight/Round	Moderate	1:25
13		Castle Moat	Round	Moderate	1:25
14		Windows and Staircases	Straight	Moderate	2:41
15		Entrance Gate	Round	Moderate	1:57
16		Guests on Horseback	Round	Fast	2:34
17	Star Home	Hall	Round	Slow	1:13
18		Library	Round	Slow/Fast	1:59
19		Kitchen	Straight/Round	Fast	3:06
20		Basement	Straight/Round	Fast/Slow	1:57
21		Bedroom	Round	Moderate	1:38
22		Studio	Straight	Moderate	2:24
23	Snow	It is snowing!	Straight/Round	Fast	1:05
24		Snow Crystals and Stars	Straight	Moderate	0:57
25		Snowstorm	Round	Fast	1:04
26		The Snow is settling	Round	Slow	2:12
27		Penguins	Straight	Moderate	1:11
28		Breaking Ice	Straight	Moderate	1:23
29		Ice Writing	Round	Fast	2:18

The resources CD

On the resources CD you will find 26 drawings (A to Z). These relate to Chapter 3, section 'Drawings on the CD-ROM'. These drawings can be used together with the 'writing sheet' or independently for other writing or drawing activities.

Also on this CD-ROM you will find several kinds of 'writing sheets', ready for use (see Chapter 3). Finally, the CD-ROM contains sheets for the Music Drawings Exercises on lines (see Chapter 4).

The book

More Write Dance is the third resource in the series.

In the first resource, Write Dance in the Nursery, we start from scratch. Quite literally. Of course, writing fully formed letters is not what matters at this stage. However, what does matter is self-expression and awareness of movements. Even the very first scratchings deserve to be taken seriously and to be stimulated by the special Write Dance nursery songs.

The second resource, simply called Write Dance (historically the first Write Dance product), helps to get the pupils ready for learning to write by making music drawings and other exercises. Using music, children are trained to complete fundamental writing movements such as 'the lazy eight'.

This third resource, More Write Dance, takes us a step further. The new Write Drawings and music drawings of this book aim to hone the finer motor skills. It is also possible to train children to form writing on lines. This book also describes how to learn to write letters following the Write Dance principles.

Contrary to Write Dance, More Write Dance does not consist of weekly themes. Instead, the practical material is grouped into three chapters called Write Drawing (Chapter Two), Learning to Write According to Write Dance (Chapter Three) and Music Drawings (Chapter Four).

Depending on their own wishes and possibilities, teachers can make their own choice from the material and put together their own programmes. More Write Dance can also be used together with any other writing method.

Summary of the chapters

Chapter One The Write Dance Philosophy

A reminder of the Write Dance philosophy with the basic Write Dance movements. All movements are linked to the books:

- Write Dance in the Nursery
- Write Dance
- More Write Dance.

Chapter Two Write Drawing, Preparing and Supporting (DVD Write Drawing)

This develops from the two earlier books from using two hands to working with the preferred hand. The exercises provided do not follow a specific order and can be used and adapted to suit the needs of the pupil. It includes sections on:

- Sensorimotor materials
- Breathing exercises
- Exercises for developing fine motor skills
- Sound word animals
- Eight Write Dance cartoons that help alternate between straight and round and the connected unbroken line.

Chapter Three Learning to Write using Write Dance (DVD Learning to Write)

Part One

The previous sections provided the skills in shape, space and movement for children to now move onto letters and words.

The chapter describes a format unique to Write Dance that is the basis of Part Two which provides both Writing Sheets and activities for each letter of the alphabet.

The Writing Sheet has a:

Movement area - the basic movement for each letter

Sound word area - this is described as phonic writing. Synchronising writing and speaking will give motor skills the attention they need and prevent the hand from 'running on ahead'.

Write drawing area - this area stimulates fun and fantasy by drawing phonic letters and crinkle sound animals.

Supplementary exercises are provided for each letter and these are called, "playing with the letter." Exercises are also provided for seven different kinds of joins, letter families, correct writing posture and moving from big to small letters.

Part Two

This provides exercises for the 26 letters of the alphabet. The left hand page provides the activities for the Writing Sheet that includes tracks from the music CD while the right hand page provides activities for "Playing with the letter".

This chapter concludes with exercises for capital letters with straight and round music.

Chapter 4 Music Drawings (DVD)

There are six Music Drawings (all have a separate section on the DVD).

Sailing Boat
Ocean Journey
Little Tea Ship
Dream Castle
Star Home
Snow.

The music tracks used in the Writing Sheets reappear in this chapter as the building blocks for the six music drawings. Writing means movement, and movement is often easier with music. Musical accompaniment creates a natural balance between tension and relaxation.

The movements are first practised without music after whole body movement, then with music building up. The drawings can be done on a variety of surfaces first before making the exercises on lines which makes a good transition to handwriting.

Final comment

The original document was written in Dutch and has been translated. The Dutch style of writing has lots of short sentences, lots of exclamation marks and no subjects. We have tried to achieve a balance, ensuring the spontaneity and creativity are upheld while still being accessible to a British market.

We hope that we have achieved what Ragnhild asked us to do:

"Let us make learning to write a real pleasure for every child!"

Chapter 1

The Write Dance Philosophy

When we write we see letters emerging from moving lines. The pen draws curves and corners in a continuous alternation of tension and relaxation. Writing is an acrobatic game of moving forward and stopping, manoeuvring and adjusting.

If we take all this activity into consideration when we write, we make the same efforts and use the same energies as, for instance, a mountain biker, a motocross racer or a slalom skier. Writing means moving, eventually using fine motor skills, but in Write Dance we prepare ourselves using gross motor skills. In the original Write Dance (and Write Dance in the Nursery) we tend to work mostly with two hands on large surfaces. Write movements come first and not the ultimate shapes. In this way the pupils can find their own rhythms and movement without yet knowing any letters.

In this book, More Write Dance, we intend to continue the spontaneity and playfulness of Write Dance, while progressing to finer motor skills and letters. We will learn the letters through the method of Write Dance, combined with games, 'Write Drawing' and music. Similar to Write Draw motifs the letters will automatically emerge from round and straight basic movements. The Write Dance circles below present an overview:

  Write Dance Circle 1 with round movements
  Write Dance Circle 2 with straight movements
  Write Dance Circle 3 with round/straight movements

Write Dance Circle One

Round basic movements and shapes

Loosening up and relaxing

In handwriting, most movements are round and they cannot be practised enough in order to develop adjustment and flexibility. We can see them emerge from the clover in the Write Dance circle, which is a combined lying eight and standing eight.

Closed movements and loops downward emerge from the upper leaf of the clover and open movements and loops upward sprout from the lower clover leaf; closed movements and loops to the left emerge from the leaf on the left and the right leaf gives us open movements and loops to the right. We will find combinations and variations on the diagonal lines which will be discussed in the chapter on Write Drawing and in 'Playing with Letters'.

While practising round movements we allow ourselves to be carried away by our own 'round', melodious sounds or by the 'round' music on the CD. Please refer to the contents at the beginning of the book that indicates which pieces of music lend themselves to round or straight movements.

All the loosening-up movements originate from the clover

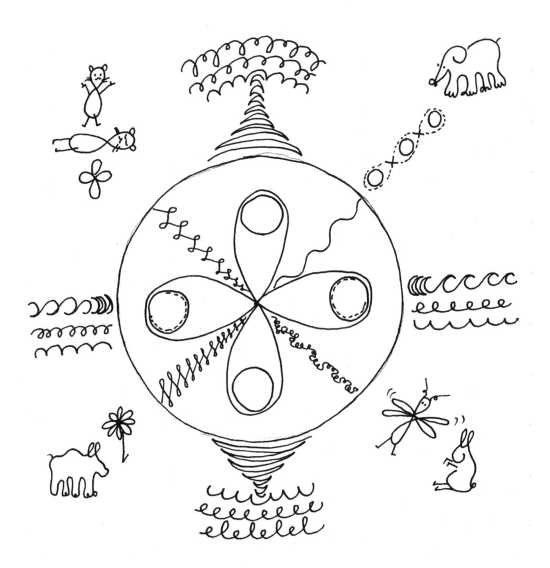

Write Dance Circle Two

Straight basic movements and shapes

Strengthening and creating tension

Straight lines and corners strengthen handwritten expressions similar to the way in which the skeleton and the muscular mass support the body. Round and straight movements, practised independently, both reappear in handwriting and unite in a resilient style of writing. Here we see the straight movements emerge from what we might call the 'Medal-Eights', in line with Write Dance Circle One. It is especially important, when learning about the capitals, to consolidate the straight basic structures first.

Without the straight exercises we would develop too much 'fat' in our handwriting. It would lead to sloppy handwriting with lazy curves. Writing v-shapes requires a decisive approach and promotes concentration. The straight exercises are ideal for counting out loud, in set tempo, with or without 'straight' music.

When the cross begins to turn you will see the round movement emerge

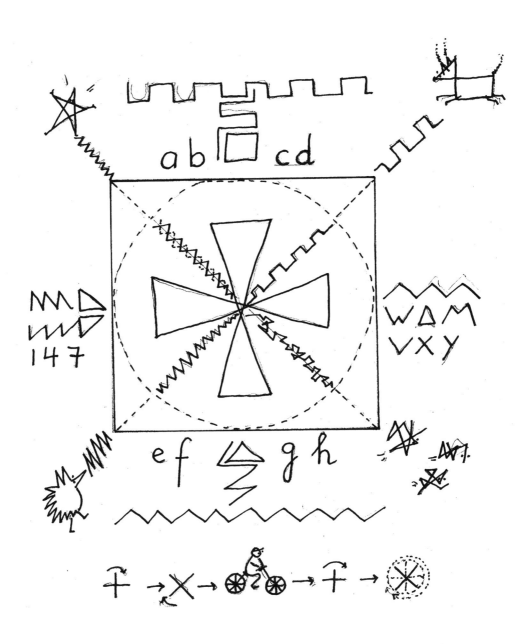

Write Dance Circle Three

Round/straight movements and shapes

Relaxation + strengthening = elasticity

Write Dance's aim is to create a smooth flowing resilient handwriting from combined straight and round movements. We see the Clover and Medal-Eights on the previous page fused into a figure with rounded corners which we could call the 'Butterfly-Eights'.

We would like the users to decide themselves how they wish to set up programmes from the materials in this book with a good mix of straight and round movements. Write Dance was built round nine themes. There are two reasons why a similar thematic structure is absent in this book:

1. Write Dance is not only used by teachers in comparable situations, but also by special needs teachers, physiotherapists, occupational therapists, dance therapists and speech therapists.

2. Not all teachers and assistants can and/or wish to progress to the same level according to the Write Dance concept, particularly with respect to the learning of letters.

Therefore the material has been presented in such a way that users can make their own easy choices in order to do the exercises in a way most suited to themselves. Write Dance invites the teacher to turn the writing process into a pedagogical, musical and didactic art that will provide the pupils with the correct dosage of writing vitamins.

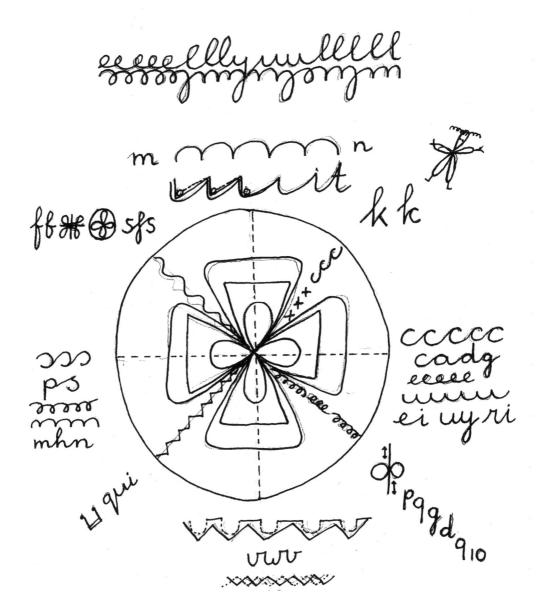

Shall we Write Dance again?

You can only hear, feel, see and experience your own rhythm, i.e. your own swing, when everything flows naturally and more or less automatically. We should imagine our rhythm as a dancing energy curve, which either twists, or straightens itself, tenses or relaxes, gives and takes, or holds and releases. There are plenty of examples of natural rhythm, for example, in ourselves, in our gait, but they can also be seen and experienced around us. Think of the waving sea, or a babbling brook. Think of the ballet of starlings or of the dance of fish. We all have those rhythmic energies in us, which lift us up, without our needing to make any conscious efforts: resign yourself to them, it happens automatically; you can relax and enjoy the experience.

Rhythm, a dancing energy, is intangible. It is a mysterious interaction of regularity and irregularity, chaos and balance. The energy concentrates itself in shapes, and then releases itself into straight or circular movements that can both attract and repel each other. Nothing is definite, everything is changeable and the same applies to handwritten expressions.

The same letter can never be drawn in exactly the same way, although some methodologies might present the situation as such.

Write Dance should be seen as an expansion of the rhythmic energy game that is called writing. You learn to write with your soul and body, your perception of the senses and personal experiences, with your fingers in shaving cream and paint, with sound words in which you can let your fantasy go... Anybody can Write Dance, with sharp or poor hearing, good or poor eyesight, few or many creative ideas, with one or two hands.

No lines or movements are considered wrong in Write Dance. You will develop your own swing naturally, experimenting with contrasts between straight and round shapes, tension and relaxation, high and low, quick and slow, inward and outward, etcetera. It is how you add your personality to the letters. Of course the letters need to be readable, but concentrating on shape perfection will only hinder progress.

Write Dance starts from the premise that if the movements and emotions are in good order, legible shapes will automatically emerge. Man has always felt the basic need to express himself in drawings and a healthy child will show the same urge clearly, from the very first chaotic scribbles at a very early age.

We tend to see more and more children wanting to write letters in their own way. And why shouldn't they? Write Dance will enable the children to investigate and experience the shapes and joins of letters in their own way.

A child is full of rhythm and movement. Writing is a form of movement, so why should we anticipate difficulties? Yet we know from experience that many children have difficulty writing and might even come to a standstill. There are all kinds of causes that we try to pre-empt in Write Dance.

In this time of computers everything moves faster and faster. Flashing images succeed each other rapidly in staccato. It can confuse the brain signals. Children who are susceptible may freeze or even become restless and hyperactive. These distress signals in children show in written expressions from an early age. Write Dance is preventative and restorative by incorporating the emotions into the scrimble, Write Drawing and writing process.

Basic Write Dance movements

Psychomotor effects
Music themes from Write Dance in the Nursery, Write Dance and More Write Dance

(Circling) round

The inner part of the circle is your psychomotor skills space
A move towards balance or liveliness and restlessness

WD in the Nursery	Pat-a-cake and Merry-go-round
Write Dance	Circles and Eights
More Write Dance	Snowstorm and Whirlwinds

Spiral

Spirals in or out
Towards or away from myself

WD in the Nursery	Pat-a-cake and Merry-go-round
Write Dance	Circles and Eights
More Write Dance	Snowstorm and Whirlwinds

Arch movement

Waving from side to side
Gentle preparation for movements in the direction
of handwriting

a. Unlooped

The movement is downward
Screening myself, inward communication

b. Looped

Starts from a circle turning clockwise
Speed and relaxation

WD in the Nursery	The Rainbow and The Gateway
Write Dance	Cats
More Write Dance	Entrance Gate and Morning

Garland movement   *Rocking from side to side*
Gentle preparation for movements in the direction of
handwriting

a. Unlooped   *The movement is upward*
Opens the centre of yourself, outward communication

b. Looped   *Starts from a circle turning anti-clockwise*
Speed and relaxation

WD in the Nursery   Little and Big Water Shute
Write Dance   The Train
More Write Dance   Little Tea Ship and Library

Ocean Wave   *Discovering the three quarter circle opening to the right and*
a move in the direction of handwriting

WD in the Nursery   Not available
Write Dance   Cats
More Write Dance   Ocean Journey and Castle Moat

Beach Wave   *Discovering the three quarter circle opening to the left and*
a move in the direction of handwriting

WD in the Nursery   Not available
Write Dance   Cats
More Write Dance   Ocean Journey and Castle Moat

| **Crinkling** | *Free, looped movements above the surface* |
| | *Flexible joins relax in all directions* |

WD in the Nursery	Kringeli-krangeli and My Dinky Car
Write Dance	A Walk in the Country
More Write Dance	Climbing Roses and Castle Moat

Waves	*Alternating arches and garlands, hills and valleys,*
	Write Dance symbolism: flowing water (Sailing Boat, Ocean
	Journey, Little Tea Ship)

WD in the Nursery	Little and Big Water Shute
Write Dance	Silver Wings over the Sea
More Write Dance	Castle Moat, Hall, Bedroom, Ocean Journey

| **Sleeping Eight** | *Subconsciousness, it is night* |
| | *Derived from two circles beside each other* |

| **Awakening Eight** | *Consciousness, eight o'clock in the morning* |
| | *Derived from two circles above each other* |

| **Clover** | *Easy crossed movements in all directions* |

| **Chain** | *Joining eights, alternated by waves and circling around* |

WD in the Nursery	Not available
Write Dance	Circles and Eights
More Write Dance	Climbing Roses and Ice Writing

Straight lines   *Vertical and horizontal, accompanied by counting*
                      Gives a sense of solidity, promotes persistence and concentration

Corners   *Sharp movements opposed to waves*
                      Write Dance symbolism: frozen water, ice crystals
                      (music drawing Snow)

WD in the Nursery   Sandy Hill and The Procession
Write Dance   The Volcano and Robot
More Write Dance   Stepped Gable, Windows and Staircases, Snow Crystals

---

Garland corner   *Gives a feeling of easy transitions between tension and*
                      relaxation
                      Encourages resilience and flexible joins

WD in the Nursery   Not available
Write Dance   Not available
More Write Dance   Sailing Boat: 'Hoisting the sails'

Chapter 2

Write Drawing, Preparing and Supporting

Write Drawing requires basic movements similar to those used for the song drawings in Write Dance in the Nursery and the music drawings in Write Dance, which are necessary to be able to write letters and words. However, the exercises in Write Drawing have moved on a step and provide a playful transition from using both hands (like we did in Write Dance in the Nursery and Write Dance) to working with the preferred hand.

It is not necessary to follow a specific order. The Write Drawing exercises can be used randomly. Of course, teachers and pupils can think of variations and adapt the exercises to suit special occasions or particular themes.

It is advisable to try the exercises with sensorimotor materials first and then move on to paper to prevent the children from using forced efforts and showing fear of failure.

Write Drawing with sensorimotor materials

Increasingly teachers find that toddlers and infants do not like to dirty their hands. Making a mess does not tend to be part and parcel of today's computer family. Yet we know that sensorial skills, motor skills and the brain develop interdependently. Sensorial experiences are essential to their development. The consolidation of movements, i.e. tracing movements repeatedly (as demonstrated in the previous books) happens automatically when working with sensorimotor materials.

Let's give an overview of the sensorimotor materials that have been mentioned in Write Dance in the Nursery.

1. Table board. The table board was introduced in Write Dance. Check that there are enough boards for all the children.

If possible have MDF sheets with a thickness of 4 to 6 cm cut to measure (60 x 42 cm). It will give boards with a surface size equal to four times A4. These measurements will also make the board suitable as a writing surface in large format (please refer to Chapter Three).

Paint the MDF boards on both sides. The required colour of blackboard paint can be made up by adding a special blackboard mixture to standard paint. Ask a painter or go to a DIY store.

- The boards are kept in place with small non-slip mats.

- In addition to chalk we can also Write Draw on the boards with sponges. Cut an average household sponge into 6 to 8 pieces and give each child working on the board two damp sponges and two dry cloths to have the best experience of wet and dry play. It is possible to make very fine lines with the tips of these sponges.

2. Slippy paints. Put a small amount of poster paint in a pump bottle with some liquid hand soap. Give it a good shake. Please have two or three colours ready for use. We will practise some finger dancing in slippy paint on a plastic tablecloth or on a plastic placemat (or on a table board).

3. Lump of clay. An alternative writing utensil. Add some liquid soap or bubble bath to a little water on the plastic tablecloth or on the plastic placemat and Write Draw in it with the lump of clay. The more water you add (from an old window cleaning spray or similar), the more the clay will spread like mud and of course you can Write Draw in it as well.

Comment: After having worked in slippy paint or with the lump of clay, it is possible to retain the Write Draw process by making a print. Place a large piece of drawing paper over it, rub it gently with your hands and the Write Draw piece of art will appear as if by magic. Making a print is a good idea because it will immediately absorb most of the paint, clay and soap. The remainder can be cleaned with cloths or kitchen roll. When the print has dried, it can be developed with chalk, crayons or felt-tipped pens.

4. Shaving cream. It is no longer necessary to use a tablecloth or placemat, as this clean lubricant can be sprayed directly onto the table. If necessary add a small drop of slippy paint for some colour. When the shaving cream becomes less slippy, spray on some water with a window spray. The table can be cleaned with two dry cloths after Write Drawing. Some children will enjoy rubbing down the table legs as well!

5. Sand. Fill a tray or an empty plastic bowl with sandpit sand or fine bird sand and Write Dance in it with your fingers.

Fingers tend to be used in slippy paint, shaving foam or sand. We could also use wooden sticks of approximately 10 cm in the slippy paint, and, if you like, you can attach small sponges to each stick with wire.

We can do some finger dancing on the table board, too. It is best to begin on a wet board and continue dancing with the fingers until the surface is dry. And then we will use chalk and sponges.

Paper

When the movements using sensorimotor materials have been consolidated it is time to move on to paper. Please vary writing utensils, moving from coarse instruments to fine ones: wax crayons, coarse felt tips, fine felt tips, colour crayons and felt-tipped pens. You will need a large amount of paper, so use large sheets, rolls of wallpaper and printer remnants.

Music

The Write Draw exercises are accompanied by music - 'round' or 'straight' music -, or sounds and noises. Let the brain hear what we are doing.

The Write Dance Area

This is the corner in the room where one or two children can Write Dance. There will be a self-made board on the wall, and there will also be table-sized boards. It is therefore possible to work on a horizontal as well as on a vertical surface. It is best to paint an old square table with blackboard paint. Don't forget the CD player.

The round Write Dance table

Use an old round kitchen table. Saw the legs at the right height, and use a jigsaw to cut a hole with a diameter of nearly 60 cm that will take a washing up bowl. Paint the table surface with blackboard paint in the required colour. Of course we will put sponges and pieces of chalk in the bowl, but when we take out the bowl a child can stand in the hole. It offers a variety of games with children round the table as well as a child in the centre.

Folding table

Paint a long board of approximately 50 cm wide using blackboard paint and attach it to the wall in such a way that it can be folded down. The legs can be folded out, too. Such a table is ideally suited for use in the PE hall where movements and write dancing can complement each other. (See the DVD section Snow.)

Computer table on wheels

It enables the Write Dance Area to be moved from classroom to classroom. All the materials listed above should be close at hand.

Write Drawing and breathing

Write Drawing could always be combined with a number of breathing exercises. Paying attention to your breathing while Write Drawing will create peace and space in the body and on the writing surface. Eventually this kind of conscious breathing will become natural; not only will the body cells acquire energy but the 'writing cells' on the writing surface will also show the signs of a healthy process of effort and relaxation. That is why singing is so healthy.

Preparatory inhaling and exhaling

We will do this exercise standing up. Put one hand on your chest and one on your tummy. Feel how your hands move up and down while breathing deeply.

Now we will inhale and stretch our arms above our heads as far as we can reach. We will breathe out, chest and stomach tucked in, and we will drop our arms slowly and bend forwards.

Breathing exercises with sensorimotor materials or on the board

Round and flat

Breathe in deeply and make your tummy round and fat. While holding your breath as long as you can, draw yourself with a fat tummy. Then release your breath and breathe normally.

Breathe out deeply and draw your tummy in tight. While holding your breath, draw yourself with a flat tummy.

Two little balloons

1. Stand in front of a wet (table-sized) board and clench both hands into fists. The fists represent two little balloons that will fly up. Inhale slowly and stretch your arms upward while the board is hanging down, and forward while the board is horizontal, keeping them approximately 10 cm above the board.

2. The balloons burst: we stretch our fingers and say: 'pow!'

3. The balloons float down: while breathing out audibly the fingers make rolling movements downward over the board.

Basic movements to the rhythm of breathing

Lay a hand on your tummy. Breathe in through your nose, expand your tummy and draw a line upward with your other hand. Breathe out through your mouth, pull in your tummy and draw a line downward. Continue like this and draw in succession:

1. A series of sharp angles or corners.

2. A series of arches.

3. A series of garlands.

Initially practise this exercise slowly and carefully. Next draw another series of angles or corners, arches and garlands, but this time making short puffs (short exhalations).

Repeat the whole exercise but switch hands: this time place your other hand on your tummy, etc. Do you feel any difference between both hands?

Balloon, on a board or on paper

Check that the board is on a non-slip mat or that the paper has been secured with masking or sticky tape. Pick up a colour crayon or a piece of chalk with your writing hand or practise this exercise by finger dancing on the wet board. Preferably allow the lower arm to rest on the table to relax the shoulder.

Blowing up

Place the writing utensil in the centre of the board or the paper. Breathe very deeply and blow up the balloon (of your stomach) and allow the pencil or piece of chalk to spiral round and round, to the left or to the right, while breathing out slowly. You can do this with your entire lower arm or only with your fingers and wrist. The balloon is growing bigger and bigger. Your lungs have almost emptied themselves and you have pumped air into the full round balloon on paper.

Releasing the air

Breathe deeply and let the pencil or piece of chalk circle round in the opposite direction while breathing out. When you are almost out of breath, the balloon (= your whole arm) will fly up in the air. Make an appropriate noise.

Try this exercise with your other hand as well. Can you feel the difference?

Variation: a square balloon

Don't move the pencil while breathing in. Draw a dash when breathing out. The dashes increase in size and are always at right angles. This is how you draw a square balloon.

Releasing the air can follow the pattern of the round balloon, but we can also use the square pattern while breathing out, working towards the centre.

Bow and arrow

We will arch the bow during a series of slow breaths in and out. Then hold your breath for a moment and shoot off some 'arrow dashes', while allowing air to escape noisily.

Also do these exercises with your other hand, allowing the arrows to shoot in the opposite direction. We will first do this exercise on the board and then on paper. Stretch your arms while shooting arrows.

Playing with Round Eights and Right Angles

The following exercises make excellent preparation for any fine motor skill writing activities which require coordination between both sides of the brain. The writing process requires perpetual crossed lines which should be done smoothly and automatically. Therefore begin with as many sensorimotor materials as possible. Always consolidate the movements by tracing them over each other many times.

After that we will change to chalk and pencil and paper. We will begin on a large sized sheet of paper, A2 or A3. If it goes well, we will move on to A4 and A5. As soon as children show signs of forced efforts and fear of failure, the teacher should allow them to experience the exercises by making big movements with one or two arms in the air or by finger dancing on the table.

The variation of large and small surfaces will develop spatial orientation and improvisation skills.

Next we will be practising the first 'round' crossing exercises which encourage relaxation and suppleness, and they will be performed to 'round' music. After that we will be trying the 'straight' crossing exercises, encouraging consolidation and concentration. We will practise these exercises to the rhythm of 'straight' music and count simultaneously.

A list of 'round' and 'straight' music is to be found at the beginning of this book. Instead of playing music you could also produce your own 'round' and 'straight' sounds. Babbeli bobbeli is 'round', but kakikukah is 'straight'.

These exercises can generally be practised with one hand, but if necessary we can also do them with both hands, in mirror image or in the same direction.

Round Eights

Lying eight, sleeping, lying

While singing a lullaby we will trace lying eights over each other. We will continue consolidation until the song is finished, keeping our eyes shut. Next we will turn it into a sleeping cat, or another sleeping animal.

Fish dance

We make our lying eights dance downward like fishes. As soon as we can perform the movement smoothly, we begin to recite opposites melodiously such as 'inward - outward', 'left - right', 'backward and forward'. Try to synchronise words and movements as much as possible.

Chinese lanterns

Create the same fluid movement as in the fish dance, but now moving from big to small. Draw a variety of Chinese lanterns in a row on a large sheet of paper and consolidate each one of them in different colours. The more colours you use, the prettier they will be. Not going smoothly? Try again in slippy paint and make a pretty print. When the print has dried, you can develop it by using colour crayons.

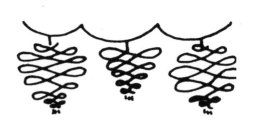

Standing eight, being awake, standing up

Start this exercise with some body writing: Draw the standing eight on your tummy and chest with one hand or both hands clasped. Extend that standing eight right to the bottom, over your feet, and to the top, over your head. Now we know what vertical stretches feel like. Next draw a standing eight and trace it a couple of times. Keep making it higher and deeper, while saying: 'high - low'.

Walking eights

The standing eight woke up completely during the previous exercise and is taking a walk. Trace each eight a couple of times before you release them. You can also do this exercise with your eyes shut or while looking up in the air. After the walk we will turn the eights into dolls or animals. (Please refer to letter S in the next chapter.)

Chain

First make a line of alternating circles and crosses. Circle around a couple of times before you cross it to turn it into a lying eight. Then circle over the second circle a few times and draw another lying eight, etcetera. If you do it correctly you will notice the wheels turning to the left and to the right in alternation. This always is an important warming-up exercise as all changes of direction proceed without interruption. Also make some waves, in other words, semi-eights.

Variation: Do this exercise in body writing with a piece of cotton wool over your eyes and ears.

Framing

This is an expansion of the Chain with some standing eights added on. Finish the pattern, always choosing the same direction. Your brains want to hear what you are doing! Therefore you should say: 'to the left' or 'to the right', 'upwards' or 'downwards'. Frame a photo or picture while doing this exercise.

Bear asleep and awake

A variation on the sleeping and wide-awake eight.

Connect all the circles with eights.

Clover in a circle

The Clover consists of two eights, a lying and a standing one. We now draw the Clover in a circle. You could first draw a standing cross with four assisting circles as supports. First consolidate the lying eight, then move on to the next standing eight in one continuous sweep, consolidating it and then moving on without stopping to the circle which will enclose the whole design. You could continue consolidating, following your own route and if you like, saying the directions: 'upwards', 'downwards', 'to the left', 'to the right,' 'all around'.

Variation: Draw the same figure in another kind of movement where garlands and arches run into each other. It will turn into a simple kolam-figure (please refer to letter X).

Semi-eight or letter S in a circle

We will start with drawing a circle. Next we will draw the vertical eight movement downward. We will draw the complementary upward movement and lift up the writing utensil. Continue to carefully consolidate this semi-eight (or letter S) a couple of times like this. It will prevent a mere straight line being drawn across the circle. Not only do you recognise the s in this figure but also the letters o and C. You can turn it into a monkey. How about a COS monkey?

Write Dance Flower

Start with tracing an upright and a diagonal cross over each other as a supporting figure. We will draw the Clover over the supporting upright cross and then draw a second Clover diagonally across. While consolidating, experiment with different changes of direction and, for instance, place the Write Dance flower in a circle.

Flowers, butterflies and dragonflies

The flower is a Clover with a stem evolving from the movement. The butterfly is a variation of the Clover, the dragonfly a variation of the Write Dance flower. After having consolidated these figures with sensorimotor materials, we will draw a big field of flowers on paper.

Letters in the Clover

It is exciting to recognise the letters in the Clover.

Start by drawing the Clover. Choose a letter, look for it in the Clover and consolidate this letter a number of times. Using sensorimotor materials such as slippy paint will increase the impact of this exercise. If you make a print on paper you will notice that it gives you the letter in mirror image.

Right Angles

The previous 'round' exercises encourage suppleness and fluid, smooth changes of direction. The following 'straight' exercises will encourage regularity and concentration. We should always count simultaneously. As soon as counting and movement are well synchronised, we will play 'straight' music. Continue to count aloud! These 'angular' movements may encourage a tendency to press too hard on the writing utensil. Allow the writing hand to have a rest and draw vertical and horizontal lines up and down.

Walking squares

Battlements

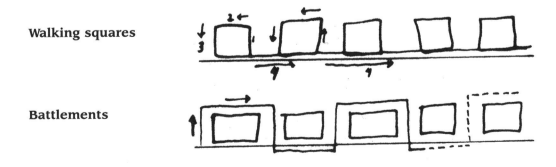

High and low battlements

Up and down the steps

Battlements and roofs

Walking triangles

Zigzags

Big and small zigzags

Little house with a cross

**Crossed houses
in a row**

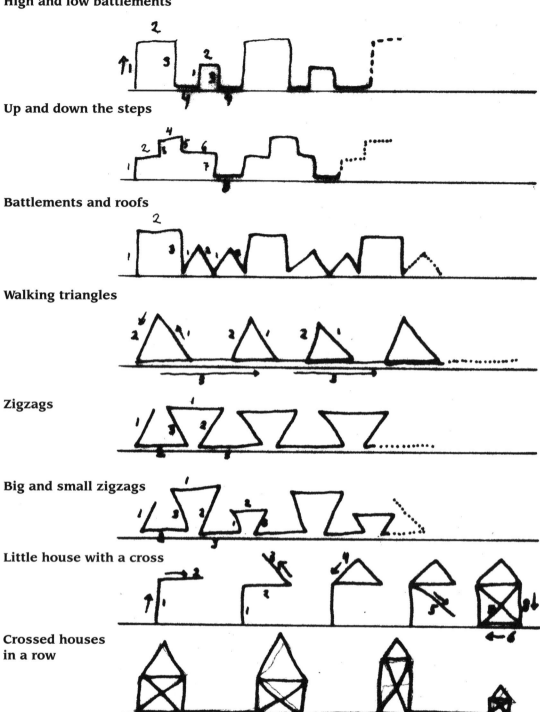

Variation: Diversify the houses and draw round shapes between them.

Marching eights

Variation: Draw alternating lines of
marching eights to 'straight' music and
walking eights to 'round' music.

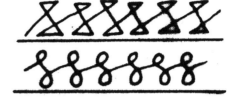

Flags

Little windmills

Medal

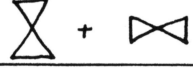

Variation: Vary the medals with Clovers,
to 'straight' and 'round' music respectively.

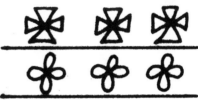

Angel with triangular wings

33

From the mountains to the sea

A succession of the four basic movements angles, arches, garlands and waves.
Consolidate these basic movements from left to right and right to left.

We have gone for a hike in the
mountains but we have forgotten our
rucksacks and need to go back.

A hare is jumping over the clumps of
grass but it has forgotten its carrot
and needs to return.

A line of dancing children: they are
holding hands and swaying from side
to side.

The waves wash over and under the
stones.

Say: 'up, down, up, down.'

And then draw all the movements one after the other in one line. Don't forget the
supportive circles.

Say: 'up down'   'hop hop hop'   'hello hello'   'bobbeli bobbeli'

You could first fold a sheet of A3 paper into 16 squares which will assure good
distribution on each line, and complete the exercise four times.

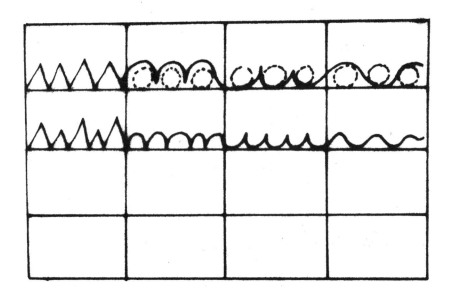

Squiggles, a Nimble-fingered Exercise

Now we have acquired the necessary amount of experience in Write Drawing, we can see how dexterous the fingers need to be and that's why we will occasionally vary write dancing with the following finger exercise.

Everybody knows the song Incy Wincy Spider when we show it climbing up the spout with our thumbs and index fingers. The fingers remain stretched.

In the following exercise we prepare ourselves for that Incy Wincy Spider movement and continue with the actual squiggles, which we will be doing with 'round' fingers. They can be the legs of a fly or a grasshopper or any other crinkle-squiggle-creature.

Read the following full description. We will stop at all the intermediate stages.

1. Two circles
Relax your shoulders and place both elbows on the table. Form two circles, one with each thumb and index finger - the sign for 'OK'.

2. Spectacles
The two finger circles touch each other, index against index, thumb against thumb. We can see the four fingers forming a pair of spectacles. If you picture the fingers as lines you will recognise the lying eights in them. Follow the lines of that lying eight with the tip of your nose.

3. A figure
Turn the two finger circles into one large opening by pushing the index fingers up and the thumbs down. What kind of figures can you see when you slowly push the fingers away from each other? A bridge, an arrow, the horns of an animal?

Repeat the bending and stretching of fingers a couple of times.

4. Lock and key
We will form another pair of circles as described in Point 1. These two circles now form a 'lock and key'. One hand does not move, while the other 'turns the key'. Keep the fingers tightly against each other; the tips of the index fingers will now touch the tips of the thumbs.

Allow the 'key' to turn round in the 'lock' repeatedly and reverse the rolls, i.e. the 'lock hand' becomes the 'key-hand' and vice versa. This is a good exercise for the wrists.

5. Relaxed, dropped shoulders
Identical to Point 4, but this time we won't stop moving one hand, instead we move both of them in opposite directions, as the lock has become a bit looser. The elbows are still resting on the table and the shoulders are relaxed. It is not easy to keep the shoulders relaxed and dropped. Exertion will often cause the shoulders to be lifted as if compensating. We also see this happen when writing or Write Drawing. The teacher or assistant can keep an eye on this.

6. Thumbs against index fingers
Make two circles according to starting position 1. The key will turn once in the lock and stop. The circles will now be opened pressing the thumbs tightly against the index fingers of the other hand. You will see a diamond, or maybe you can recognise some other shapes?

7. Ten stretched legs

Starting with this diamond shape we will now allow the lower thumb and index finger to be released and we turn them upward in the opposite direction where they will meet again. If you keep repeating this, it will give you the same Incy Wincy Spider movement with stretched fingers or legs.

8. Ten crooked squiggly legs

The elbows are resting on the tabletop, the shoulders are relaxed. This time we are not doing the Incy Wincy spider movement with stretched fingers, but with well bent fingers. Vary the pace and accompany the legs with rising and falling insect noises. The finger movements and the vibrations of the vocal chords are synchronised. Stop and stand, 'sh-sh-sh-shushing' and 'cri-cri-cri-cking'! Mind the upper part of your body: are the shoulders well relaxed? Check your breathing and breathe deeply a couple of times.

Thumbs and index fingers are now rolling and tumbling over each other effortlessly. You could count along, up to ten, twenty, thirty...

9. Clean all the legs

Relaxed upper part of the body, elbows on the table, fingers bent. There are a couple of other legs that need cleaning. The thumbs now move across to the middle fingers, which should be repeated several times. The ring fingers are next in line to be given a good wash or prod. Finally it's the little fingers' turn.

Allow the thumbs to walk slowly over all your finger tips. Do not forget to keep the fingers rounded.

Have you kept the upper part of you body relaxed and have you remembered to take the occasional deep breath?

It means you have become a fully-fledged crinkle-squiggle-creature!

It does not need telling that these fine motor skill exercises keep the brain in motion!

Crinklidong and sound-word animals

Letters are shapes that evolve from movements. Suppleness of movement is necessary to be able to form successful shapes. In the next series of exercises we will start with the movements and then see how individual shapes emerge.

Crinkling in slippy paint to music

In Write Dance the theme A Walk in the Countryside introduced us to crinkling. Crinkling means making fluid, looped and unbroken movements across the writing surface, in any direction, in whatever way you feel is right. Crinkling is in preparation of cursive writing. We will repeat this kind of crinkling to the music in the Hall in Starhome, the music drawing.

We will first crinkle in slippy paint and then make a print on paper. That is how we acquire the basics for our crinkle creature. Let your print dry and then develop it with other types of writing utensils: pieces of chalk, felt tips, colour crayons, fine liners... Be inspired by your crinkle drawing: follow the lines and turn it into a crinkle animal with eyes, ears, legs, whiskers, etc.

We can cut out our crinkle animal and stick it on coloured cardboard. Alternatively we can enlarge and shrink it on a photocopier, which will give us an entire family to cut out and if you like they can be laminated. Hang them up and turn them into a mobile, or glue them onto sticks and work out a shadow play with puppets.

Remember your own crinkle animal

Draw a crinkle animal. Try with a finger on a wet plate. Follow the movements of direction with your finger and say them out loud: 'Upwards', 'downwards', 'to the left', 'to the right,' diagonally', etc. If the concepts of left and right are too difficult, say something like ' to the door' and 'to the window'. Repeat it a number of times, also with your eyes closed and thus remember the movements that constitute your crinkle animal.

Now take a big sheet of paper. Can your remember the directions and do you still remember and feel the loops? First try them on the empty sheet of paper dancing with your fingers and with your eyes closed. Then take a piece of chalk or a pencil and draw your own personal crinkle animal with your eyes open and this time a real one.

Distorting mirrors

Once you have got to know your crinkle animal well, you can also draw it in other shapes, as if facing a distorting mirror. It will make everything really long and thin, or simply very short and fat.

That is how we experiment with shapes and movement.

Crinkle-word-animals

You can turn any word into a crinkle-word-creature. For instance, take your own name or a phonic word from the following chapter. Each crinkle-word-creature has a head and a tail. We will start with the tail and draw it crinkling in the air. We will add the word to it without interrupting our writing movement, followed by a crinkly nose or head. Next we allow the movement to make its way back to connect head and

tail with plenty of imagination. Repeat this, but this time with chalk on the board or with crayons or pencils on paper. Add eyes and ears and legs.

This exercise makes us feel that writing a word is no more difficult than drawing a crinkle creature. Movements lead to shapes and a shape is derived from the movement.

Variation: We would initially associate crinkling with fluid, round movements. For variation and contrast it is fun to draw some crinkle-word-creatures with sharp, angular movements. We will add some 'angular' noises, counting, or playing 'straight' music.

Eight Write Dance Cartoon figures

Ellybelly   Rodoggy   Crinklina   Crickle   Bibby   Hoggy

Sitari boy   Sitari girl

The importance of the cartoon figures is how to alternate between straight and round, and the connected unbroken line. The cartoon figures have been designed to have set shapes as well as flexibility. In my experience the cartoon figures are stimulating because children feel attracted to animals and cartoons. The cartoon figures are not difficult and it is possible to incorporate a personal expression in many different ways. It encourages self-confidence.

Always first draw the cartoon figures holding one hand up in the air. Then make them while finger dancing on the tabletop, or with sensorimotor materials. Only then change to the table board with a sponge and a piece of chalk, or to a (large) sheet of paper with wax crayons and colour pencils. Consolidate them many times over each other!

There are round and straight cartoon figures as shown above. We will look at the eight of them in turn.

Ellybelly

An elephant with crinkly legs.

Basic outline in five steps:

Step 1

Say: 'ear, ear, ear'

Step 2

'head, head, head'

Step 3

'trunk, trunk, trunk'

Step 4

'body, body, body'

Step 5

'leg, leg, leg, leg, tail'

After the basic outline has been completed, we will connect the ear, trunk, lower head, first, second, third and fourth leg, and finish with the rear and back. We will complete this joining in one line as much as possible and we will say the parts of the body out loud. The tail will be drawn separately.

At first the children tend to go round and round at the bottom of the trunk and underneath the legs. It does not matter, because as they become more experienced they will draw a real crinkly trunk and crinkly legs by combining arches and garlands.

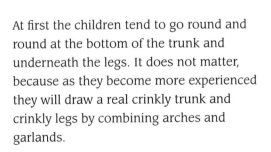

Rodoggy

Rodoggy is a robot dog with aerials on its ears and tail. He is the angular companion of the round Ellybelly and can protect him from danger.

Basic outline in four steps:

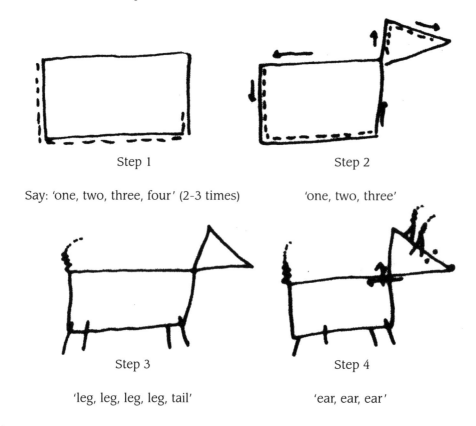

Step 1	Step 2
Say: 'one, two, three, four' (2-3 times)	'one, two, three'

Step 3	Step 4
'leg, leg, leg, leg, tail'	'ear, ear, ear'

When the basic outline is drawn, we will choose another colour and connect body and head and count up to seven.

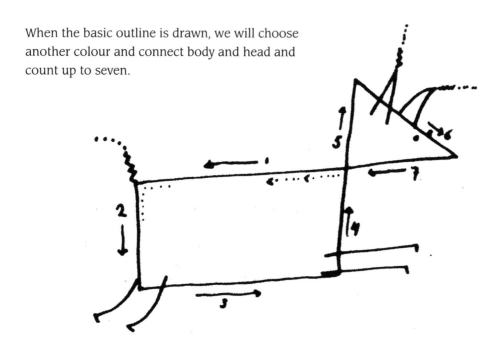

Crinklina

Crinklina is a big, round animal with the ears of a rabbit, the snout of a pig and the lump of a dromedary.

Basic outline in six steps:

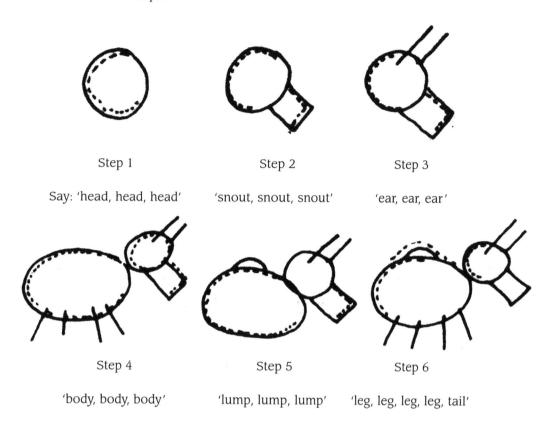

Step 1	Step 2	Step 3
Say: 'head, head, head'	'snout, snout, snout'	'ear, ear, ear'

Step 4	Step 5	Step 6
'body, body, body'	'lump, lump, lump'	'leg, leg, leg, leg, tail'

When the basic outline is drawn, we will choose another colour and connect head and body, starting with the ears.

Crickle

A flying, cricketlike figure, the angular companion of Crinklina. When there is danger she warns Crickle with her cree-cree-noises. Each new Crickle you draw will be totally different!

We do not need a basic outline: its body, head and wings consist of eight joined, straight lines in total. We will draw it in two steps:

Step 1	Step 2
Count from 1 to 8	Say: 'leg, leg, eye, eye'

The pen glides along with the voice! Counting and drawing lines happen synchronically.

Although it is not difficult to draw straight lines, there might be pupils who do not dare to cross the lines.

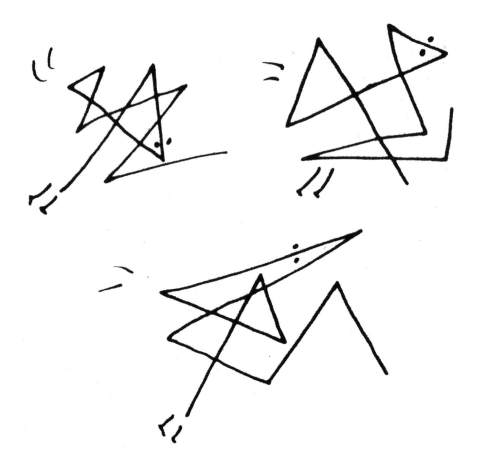

Bibby

Bibby is a little rabbit that sometimes looks forward, sometimes to the right, and sometimes to the left.

The basic outline is a standing eight with two ears:

Bibby looks forward   Bibby looks to the left   Bibby looks to the right

Say out loud: 'nose, ear, ear, right down to the bottom, stop'

The tail of the left-right-figure can be drawn
separately, or be joined up in the movement downwards.

Can you draw two Bibbies simultaneously?

They are angry and are back to back.   But when they look at each other they are friends.

Hoggy

Hoggy is Bibby's best friend. And yet they are quite different. Bibby is round all over, while only Hoggy's tummy is round, but for the rest Bibby consists of many sharp angles. Hoggy is an inquisitive little animal that cannot keep its nose out of anything. While writing letters Hoggy's nose points exactly where you still need to pay some extra attention (please refer to next chapter).

The basic outline is oval:

Count aloud from 1 to 6   continue saying: 'hacky-tacky, hacky-tacky...tummy'

Sitari (boy and girl)

The name Sitari is a phonic word consisting of the existing zither (the musical instrument) and star (and the English word 'star'.) Sitari is a radiant personality and loves music. While copying letters Sitari looks for letters and words which have been most successful.

In fact there is not one Sitari but there are two. Brother and sister. The brother is made out of straight lines, the sister is made of loops.

The basic outline is a capital A with a long stroke across:

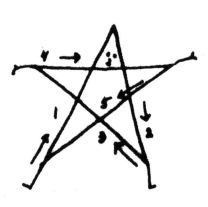 

Sitari boy   Sitari girl

Count aloud from 1 to 5:   You do not need to count while drawing Sitari girl
                                because she consists of one continuous line.

The DVD

Write Drawing

This section of the DVD illustrates some of the areas identified in the text including:

Write Dance cartoon figures

Ellybelly

Rodoggy

Crickle

Crinkle word animals

Write drawing with slippy paints - sensorimotor materials

Write drawing and breathing

Capital letters accompained by straight and round music.

Chinese lanterns

Cos Monkey (Semi-eight or letters in a circle)

Write Dance Flower.

Chapter 3

Learning to Write Using Write Dance

Write Dance considers writing to be more than just writing letters and words with a pen or pencil on paper. For instance, we can also 'write' with sensorimotor materials. And what we write initially does not necessarily have to look like letters and words. Learning to write using Write Dance has already been given extensive coverage in Write Dance in the Nursery, Write Dance and in the previous chapter Write Drawing. Now that we are actually moving on to letters and words we can reap the benefits of all the previous exercises. We have spent a considerable amount of time on shape, space and movement in order to achieve successful letters and words. Moreover we have taught the children to manage their personal ways of expression, both in their space and on the writing surface.

Learning to write using Write Dance means:

- Learning to write, developing your own style and rhythm.
- An immediate workout of your personal cursive writing style.
- Writing on a copied or folded writing sheet (A3 or A4 or table board).
- Consolidation and sound writing.
- Playing with the letters.

The writing sheet

Writing sheets make a practical tool when learning to write letters. They are not just about writing individual letters, but more about joining them into sound words. Each writing sheet is a combination of warm-up movements, focused writing exercises and Write Drawing pictorial letters and crinkle words. Therefore a writing sheet will always consist of three areas: movement area, sound word area and Write Drawing area.

A Writing Sheet

(Movement area)

(Sound word area)

(Write drawing area)

This introduction will be followed by an alphabetical section in which each one of the 26 letters will be discussed on two pages, side by side: a page on the left and a page on the right. The right-hand pages will always be titled 'Playing with the Letter'. The left-hand pages contain instructions how to complete the writing sheet. The division of the writing sheet into three areas will be discussed in the section 'How to make the writing sheets'.

The movement area

The teacher first demonstrates the basic movements in the air. Because of the direction of our script, from left to right, it is best if the teacher faces the front away from the class. The children will copy the movements and continue, finger dancing on the desks. Matching sounds can be made up or a short piece of music can be played according to the suggestion on the left-hand page of the alphabetical part.

The children will then make these basic movements visible on the writing sheet with their writing utensils. The teacher will do this on the big board. This area may look quite messy because the main purpose is warming up!

Now we are ready to write in the sound word area. We could practise the Writing Posture Rhyme first (see below).

The sound word area

The sound word area consists of four writing lines of which each one has been subdivided by means of nine dots. The section How to make the writing sheets describes how to divide the sound word area yourself. Teachers will draw their own writing sheets on the big board and demonstrate writing in the sound word area.

A letter can be placed on each dot. The division of four lines with nine dots will encourage the pupils to use the space well and make big letters.

On the first line we will write the intended letter nine times, on the three following lines we will write the sound words. We have given some very simple sound words in the alphabetical part on the left-hand pages. For letter e we have given el and ele, for letter f we have given fa and faf.

On the left-hand page of letter f we see the following scene with 4 x 9 = 36 letters:

ff ff ff fff
fa fa fa faf
fa fa fa faf
fa fa fa faf

The underlined letters indicate the sound words. These examples have been typed, because in practice the children will all create their own letters. If the example is too difficult at this stage, or if there are any other difficulties, adapt it by leaving out the final letter, for instance, fa fa fa fa. Or make other vowel and consonant combinations. Each letter in the alphabetical section on the left-hand page will be accompanied by a particular join. Seven types of joins are explained later in this chapter.

Important!

We have the choice of starting to write individual letters: looped letters without a loop (l), or to start with writing loops immediately and joining up (2). In both cases the sound words should be traced over each other a few times, each time using a different colour, which will give us beautiful 'rainbow words'. This should not be done precisely or accurately, but with the intention of finding your own style and rhythm. The writing sheet is a work sheet, and therefore it may look colourful, so that you can see that the writer has been extremely busy.

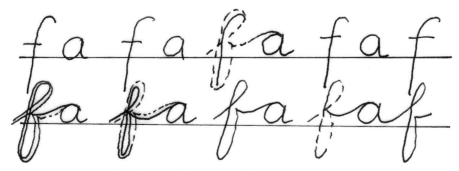

sound writing and its consolidation into rainbow words

Sound words should be spoken as we write them. This is called sound writing. Sound writing is very important and if necessary the teacher should continue to encourage the children to make sounds. Synchronising writing and speaking will give motor skills the attention they need and prevent the hand from 'running on ahead'.

As soon as the pupils have become acquainted with the letters and joins, we can be less strict in the sound word area and find phonic rhythms such as:

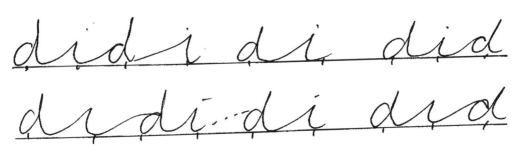

didi di did   or   dididi did

It is important to write sound words consisting of 4 letters at an early stage, so that the consonant does not always appear at the beginning and at the end of the word, but also in the middle. Moreover, words such as *didi* and *bebe* are beautiful names for crinkle-word animals.

If we allow ourselves to be carried along by a sound rhythm while writing, the writing and phonic images are more likely to be engraved in our memory. Your brains like to hear what you are writing!

Note: While writing in the sound area we do not use any music because the music is in the voice.

The Write Drawing area

The purpose of this area is to stimulate their fantasy and to continue fun in writing by drawing pictorial letters and crinkle sound word animals. In the alphabetical part you will find an illustration of the accompanying pictorial letter by the side of each letter on the left-hand page. The pictorial letters are so simple that the teacher will be able to draw them on the board without any difficulty.

Pictorial letters and sound word animals will create an expressive and personal relationship with the letters. All these figures can be expressed with movements and inspire us to make up stories, for instance, 'Mr V says good morning to the vava' or 'pepe and keke are going to swim'.

Drawings on the CD-ROM

The following are some examples of the 26 drawings which have been saved on the CD-ROM.

These drawings or parts of them can serve as examples for Write Drawing on the writing sheet. But it is also possible to use the drawings independently without the writing sheets. When making a print-out these drawings will always be at the top of an A4 sheet with the rest of the sheet remaining empty. The drawing can be coloured in, which will help consolidate the movements. And the drawings can help provide inspiration for Write Drawing in the empty space.

The drawings can be laminated and collated into a booklet to be left out in the Write Dance area.

C

S

b

l

j

Seven types of joins

In the alphabetic part you will always find the handwritten letter on the left-hand page, including the basic movements from which it originates. The handwritten letters are not meant to be precise instructions. It is possible to adapt the shape of the letter; moreover both teacher and pupils add their own style and rhythm to the letters, particularly by means of the variables big / small, wide / narrow and full / thin. Of course the letters should be written clearly and well, combining straight and round movements.

While joining up we will try to achieve a healthy alternation of straight and round shapes to develop suppleness and elasticity. Involuntary straight and sharp letters, because motor skills have not allowed the pupil to manage the round principle adequately, will inevitably lead to forced elongated letters and unintentional strokes. When learning the joins, the straight and the round should be given equal chances.

In the following overview all the joins I have identified will be discussed and my suggested joins can be found for each letter on the left-hand pages of the alphabetical part.

Sailing Boat join: a d h i m n r (t) u

This join has been named after the music drawing Sailing Boat.

The Sailing Boat join consists of a rounded angle emerging from the garland. A frequent repetition of the music drawing The Sailing Boat enables us to consolidate this rounded sharp join (see DVD).

Little Tea Ship join: c e l x (k)

The Little Tea Ship join has been named after the music drawing The Little Tea Ship. We use this join for letters that are round at the bottom and encourage a rounded join to the following letter.

While practising the music drawing The Little Tea Ship we can make deep as well as shallow garlands. The deep garland is needed for e.g. the letters u, v and w. We need the flat garland for the Little Tea Ship join.

Letter k acquires a rounded join if we write it with an ocean wave. If not, the k will have a sharp join (see DVD).

Good morning join: b (f) o (t) v w

These letters are joined to the next letter by a flexible horizontal line, with or without a small loop. Letters o, v and w need the good morning join at the top of the letter; it is as if we are making a salute or touching our caps. Letters b, f and t need the good

morning movement to begin half way; it is as if we are shaking hands at that point. We have seen that the sailing boat join can also link the t at the bottom. Later we will see that the letter f can also be joined up by the lower loop.

Beach wave join: p   s

We were introduced to ocean waves in Write Dance where Cats are the theme. Ocean waves are basic movements for the letters a, c, d, g and q. However, when the ocean waves reach the beach, they fall over because they are thrown back. They then become beach waves. The beach wave is a basic movement for the letters p and s; we call the type of join for these two letters the beach wave join.

Sharp corner join: (k)   q

There are children who draw sharp corner joins where they should not. The cause is a delayed development of their motor skills. A sharp corner join is however possible for the letters k and q.

As shown above: rounding the sharp angle of the k into an ocean wave, gives it a rounded join.

Lower loop join: (f)   g   j   y

Lower loop and lower loop joins merge into each other. The lower loop is a semi-eight or an extended arch.

If the lower loop of the letter f emerges from a garland, the f will be joined with the good morning join.

Wave join: z

In Write Dance we practised the waves in the theme Silver Wings. The music drawing Ocean Journey in More Write Dance also allows us to practise all kinds of waves: 'ordinary' waves, ocean waves and beach waves.

The wave join, based on the ordinary wave only occurs in the letter z.

Letter families and sound word families

The letters are ordered alphabetically in the letter part, but that does not mean that the pupils will write the sound words in alphabetical order. The order below takes into consideration the family likenesses from a motor skill point of view. Teachers are free to choose a different order, or to make sound words themselves which might arise from a reading method.

The Garland Family   e   i   l   o   t

el   the e as well as the l are the results of looped garlands which we practised in the Train in Write Dance and will therefore not create any difficulties.

it   the i as well as the t are the results of an unlooped garland which changes into the sailing boat join.

te   the two letters that are known to us. The t could be joined to the e by means of a good morning join, a continuation of the crossed bar in t.

ot   the o is a closed shape starting to the left like the garland and has the same movement feature as the e.

Cat Family (ocean waves)   c   a   d   g   q

The opening letters will always contain an ocean wave. Take note of the join with the following letter.

ce   rolls on nicely with the little tea ship join.
at   sailing boat join.
di   sailing boat join.
gi   lower loop.
qe   sharp corner join.

Strong legs family (lower loops)   j   y   (g)

jo

yl   goes down very deep and up very high. It invites you to try it out with your body.

Arch family   m   n

me

nu   two new letters at the same time, but in mirror image. The n is an arch and the u is a garland.

The deep and shallow garland family   u   r

ur   The deep garland of the u as well as the shallow garland of the r can be practised with the Little Tea Ship.

ra

Rabbit ears family (upper loops)   l   h   k   b

la

hi

ke

be

Upper and lower loops   f

fa

The oval family   v   w

va

wo

The beach wave family   p   s   x

pe

su

xi   the x consists of an ocean wave as well as a beach wave.

Wave

Ze

Additional comments for the use of writing sheets

The writing sheets are work sheets that can be used in various different ways: they could offer a first introduction to letters, but they could also be used to reinforce skills.

The writing sheets are a flexible tool while learning to write and they simultaneously support reading and a good pronunciation.

Writing book

If you like, writing on writing sheets can be combined with writing in an exercise book from the start. On the writing sheet we consolidate with several colours, making rainbow words, but we will not do so in the exercise book. There we write in one single line.

Special books with wide lines of approximately 1.5 cm (0.6 inch) are preferable for young children. Give your pupils plenty of space! If there are not any wide-lined books available ask them to skip lines. Or use the sheets on the CD-ROM.

File

The writing sheets can be put and kept in a personal file together with Write Drawings and music drawings.

Assessment

The teacher will see immediately if the space has been used well and if motor skills have developed sufficiently. If that is not so, it would be advisable to pay some attention to them at another time, e.g. by using sensorimotor materials.

It would be fun to put Sitari, the pentagonal star man next to the most successful detail on the writing sheet and to place a Hoggy nose where some improvement might be welcome. The teacher could ask the children to do the same in their own books, or in someone else's.

Comment: If Sitari's pentagonal star is too difficult for a small drawing, they could draw a little round face instead.

Playing with letters

The left-hand pages of the alphabetical part contain instructions how to complete the writing sheets. On the right-hand pages you will always find some playful exercises to support the learning process of forming letters.

The exercises on the right-hand pages vary in character. The exercises in mirror image are meant to help distinguish the letters b, d, g, p and q, which are so confusing for children. It is best to try these exercises in mirror image with the aid of sensorimotor materials. In addition to the exercises in mirror image there are some other exercises to practise distinction, e.g. Anna and Okky for the letters a and o.

You will nearly always find an exercise with the pictorial letter.

There are also exercises that allow us to experiment with different versions of one particular letter (f, p, r and s).

The teacher will make a choice from the exercises on the right-hand pages. The drawings on the CD-ROM are connected with the illustrations that go with Playing with letters.

Face and body

The letter g is accompanied by a body writing exercise described on the right-hand page. (See also Chapter 2, Write Drawing: Chain.) Other letters, too, could be written on the face or body (or in the air, in front of the body).

upper

middle

lower

Comment: Writing for instance a letter b on your face or up in the air is a good variation of the mirror image exercises. The spectator will regard your b as a d!

Close your eyes

If we write with our eyes shut, it makes us aware of any little change in the movements and they become really heartfelt. If the eyes are too critical, they slow down the movement. It will always be an educational and exciting experience to write the sound words on the table board with your eyes open, then with your eyes shut. What kind of result did you get? Wider or narrower? Smaller or bigger? Etcetera

Letter poster

A self made letter poster will be far more fun than a printed one. Take a large piece of paper, divide it into 24 squares (e.g. six rows of four) and draw a pictorial letter (one you invented) in each square. The m and n will be together in one square and so will be the v and w.

How to make the writing sheet

If we want to use our table-sized board as a writing sheet, we will have to divide the board into fields, lines and dots. It is a good exercise, which will encourage eye-hand-coordination and will give us a vision of the entire writing surface. If we work on paper, it will not be necessary to make each individual writing sheet, as we can copy or print an example from the CD-ROM. Now and then it is useful however, also with an eye to fine motor skills, to fold and divide your own writing sheet.

The division in three areas

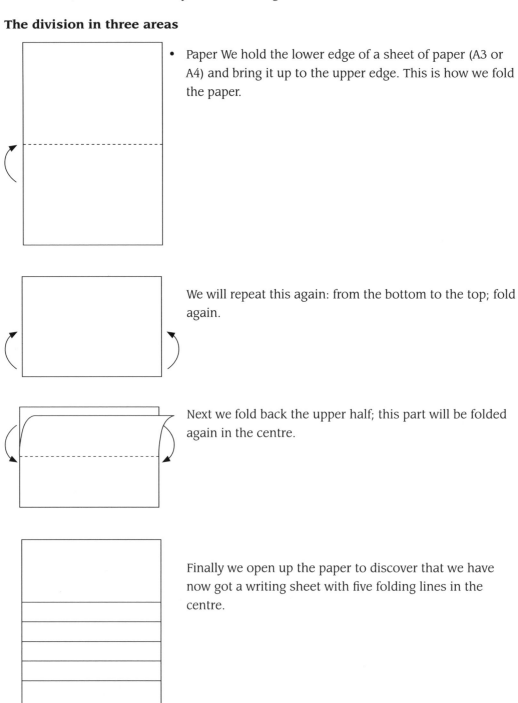

- Paper We hold the lower edge of a sheet of paper (A3 or A4) and bring it up to the upper edge. This is how we fold the paper.

We will repeat this again: from the bottom to the top; fold again.

Next we fold back the upper half; this part will be folded again in the centre.

Finally we open up the paper to discover that we have now got a writing sheet with five folding lines in the centre.

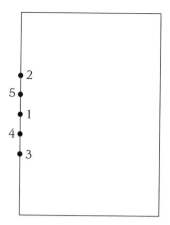

- Table board. Place the table board on a non-slip mat, so that it does not move. When dividing the board we can't fold it but we will divide it intuitively.

  We will run our fingers along one of the long edges of the board, while we sing: 'Where is the centre? 'Where is the centre? Put a dot here.' The index finger of the non-writing hand will rest on a spot which has become the centre. The writing hand will now place a dot with a sponge or a piece of chalk.

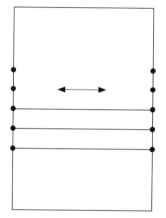

We will repeat this procedure until we have five dots.

Next we place the corresponding dots on the other side at the same height. We could do this in the same way as we did before (but now on the opposite side of the board), or by moving the index finger of the writing hand from side to side horizontally. We call it line dancing, in preparation of drawing lines.

Drawing writing lines (boss and assistant)

- If we use the table board, we will draw five lines between the dots on either side. If we use paper we will draw lines on the five folding lines.

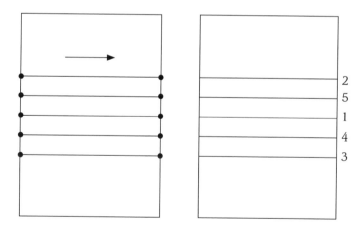

- First just do some line dancing, before you draw a line. Drawing a line with a wet sponge on the table board is not particularly difficult. Just do a bit more line dancing and dry the line.

- Drawing the lines with chalk or pencil at the start tends to be less simple than drawing with the sponge.

- Writing on paper means both hands have a function, not only the writing hand, although of course the writing hand is the boss. The non-writing hand plays a part, too, because it is the assistant. It needs to slide the paper into the right position, hold it in place as long as necessary, and then move it on again, etc.

Even at this stage, drawing the writing lines, the assistant will help out by placing the writing sheet at a convenient angle. It is best for right-handed children to pull the writing sheet a little to the left, so that the lines are drawn upwards in a slightly diagonal line.

It is convenient for those who are left-handed to draw the lines slightly towards themselves, downwards in a slightly diagonal line. In order to do so left-handed pupils will need to turn the writing sheet slightly to the right.

- Try to practise drawing the five lines holding the writing hand in the air, quickly and immediately.

- Try line dancing with your eyes shut which will give you the best sense of what is happening.

- Turn the table board or paper 45 degrees in order to draw the lines towards you.

Putting nine dots on the writing lines

We might have drawn five lines, but as shown in the example, we will only use four as writing lines. On each of those four lines we will now place nine dots.

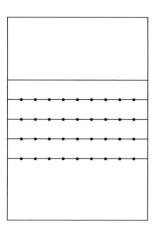

- We will leave a small margin on both sides of the writing line, as wide as the index finger of your non-writing hand, the assistant. It will bring us to dots 1 and 2.

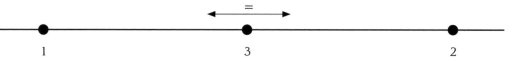

- The assistant's index finger moves from side to side accompanied by the sung words 'Where is the centre, where is the centre, put a dot here' and stops in the centre. The writing hand (boss) places a dot: dot 3.

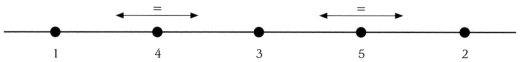

- We arrive at dot 4 and dot 5 in the same manner...

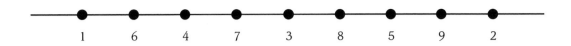

- And finally at dots 6, 7, 8 and 9. You simply cannot go wrong.

- We will always start by placing nine dots on a writing line, and then we put dots on the other lines. We can do this either by repeating the procedure above, or by placing dots under each other.

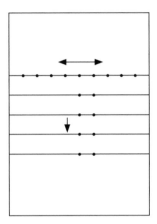

The Writing Posture Rhyme

Any teacher will know that pupils will benefit from a correct posture.

A bad posture encourages cramp in your hand, caused by fatigue and it will not produce good writing results. The purpose of the writing posture rhyme is to encourage the pupils to take on a good writing posture.

Prior to writing in the sound word area it is always a good idea to have a quick run through of the writing posture rhyme. We are sitting in our places, holding the writing utensil in our writing hands, with the writing sheet in front of us.

The rhyme is as follows:

> **1 Stamp your feet**
> **2 Bang your knees**
> **3 Shake your body**
> **4 Grab your writing hand and... ho!**
> **5 Let the assistant have a go**
> **6 Measure the distance eye to sheet**
> **7 And put your hand there nice and neat**
> **8 Take your pen and balance it steady**
> **Please don't squeeze, it makes me giddy!**

Clarification:

1. Quickly stamp your feet.

2. Give the knees a quick shake against each other.

3. Shake your whole body, also your arms and hands.

4. The assistant (the non-writing hand) grasps the lower arm of the writing hand, lifts it up from the table and drops it on the word ho, so that you can feel the lower arm fully resting on the table. The elbow should preferably stick out a little over the edge.

5. The assistant now slides the writing sheet into its final position and turns it to the right, similarly to drawing lines: a little to the left for right-handed pupils, a little to the right for left-handed people. Now the assistant can stroke the writing arm a couple of times, from shoulders to wrist, to encourage its boss.

6. Place the assistant's index, middle and ring fingers against the forehead and place the elbow back on the table. The distance from the eyes to the paper is just right: at an elbow's length and this will be easy to memorise while writing and just as easy to remember. Some will measure the distance with a 'long nose', but that will make little difference to the distance from eyes to sheet.

7. Now drop the assistant arm in a relaxed manner, below the writing sheet. While writing, the assistant can change position and move over to the top of the writing sheet.

8. Move your fingers, stretch them and bend them, and play a little with the writing. instrument.

(While holding the pencil in you hand you could practise the squiggles from the chapter Write Drawing.)

Playing with (sound) words

When all the letters have had a turn and have been put into practice using very simple words such as ata, bebe, cece, etcetera, it is time to introduce some variation in the word pictures. Please find some suggestions below, which could be adjusted and expanded at any time.

For the time being we will be using a writing sheet with a movement area and a Write Drawing area. The movement area will require some practice in basic movements and Write Drawing will provide a creative conclusion, using the new sound words as a source of inspiration. Once upon a time there was a sune that met a nesu in the woods.

The writing book (preferably with wide lines) should always be close at hand. Words can be noted down without tracing them this time, just use a grey pencil. Giving them an exercise book with wide lines to work in will help the children find their own swing in shapes, movements and space division.

Pupils without enough support in a wide-lined exercise book, particularly with regard to the three areas, might benefit from using a copied 'notebook sheet' (please refer to CD-ROM) which shows the limits for the upper and lower zones, drawn with a ruler.

Linking sounds

To start with we will present a couple of variations on sound words with four letters, which we will write in pairs on a line with nine dots, the middle dot remaining empty:

- The well-known sound words, but this time with other vowels:

  didi dada

  dida dadi

  bebe bobo
  etc.

- To make a sound word yourself, please reverse the syllables:

  lama mala

  tibo boti

  sune nesu
  etc.

- We will begin the following word with the last syllable of the previous word:

mela lama

mani nita

tobi bidu

dujo joby
etc.

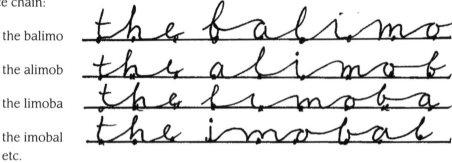

We can also make sound words of six letters, vowels and consonants alternating each other. If you continue to remove the first letter and place it at the end, it will produce a nice chain:

the balimo

the alimob

the limoba

the imobal
etc.

Comment: Writing such a long word is quite a challenge. We trace them, making rainbow words and do not expect all six letters to be joined at once. Pupils will discover themselves what is the easiest way for them to write long words.

Three words in a row

We will make up a sentence and pick out the four keywords, each one consisting of three letters. The four words will be written on lines below each other, and each one will be repeated twice on the same line. For example: 'Tonight the man will fry a big egg. We will pick out the words: man   fry   big   egg

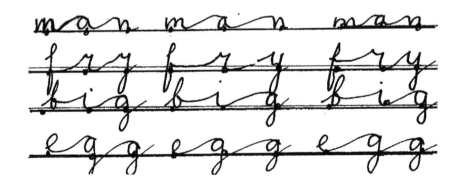

Of course you could reverse the order and use four words to build a story.

For example: day   cat   may   bed

                      eat   jar   out   jam

                      owl   eat   fly   out

Imaginary words with double consonants

All the letters will be discussed in the sound words on the left hand pages, but the vowels will receive more practise because they occur in several sound words. We will bring out the consonants as follows:

Double a consonant with one vowel preceding and one vowel following. It will create an imaginary word of four letters. Write the word twice on a writing line, not using the central dot. This is a way to practise consonants.

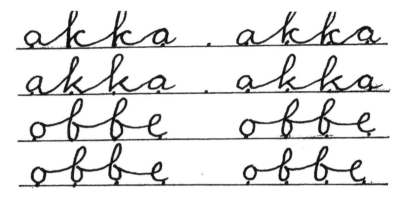

Variation: Now finish with a variety of consonants on the empty dots. What kind of animals have you created? What are the animals of the other children in your class?

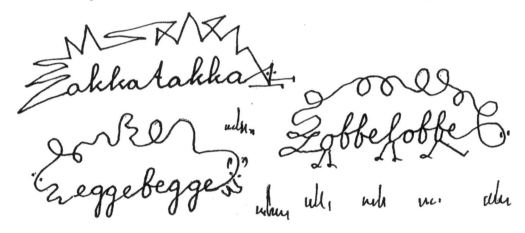

Sailing ship join exercise

a   d   h   i   m   n   r   t   u

Make words and sentences only using these letters. It will give you an excellent idea how to use the sailing ship joins.

69

Moving from big to small letters

The writing areas of the copied or folded A4 sheet are approximately 35 mm wide and give a child practising early writing enough space to try out their fine motor skills. It is important to write big letters on the nine dots to develop flexing and stretching muscles. The letter in the central zone may range from 10 mm to 15 mm.

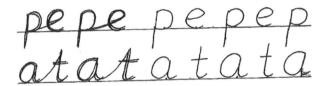

When the child is older she will automatically feel the need to write smaller letters.

At that stage we will be able to halve the distance between the writing lines on the writing sheet, and on each writing line we will add another 8 dots between the 9 existing dots (this advanced writing sheet is on the CD-ROM). It will give us a picture with eight lines and 17 dots each. The letters in the central zone will be approximately 6-8 mm high which matches the size of the letters in the wide line book. It is possible to repeat the simple sound word suggestions several times with these 17 dots as 'scale exercises', but in this space division it would be more attractive to write small sentences, or longer columns with existing words.

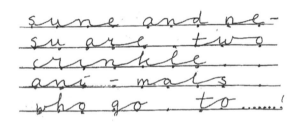

The dot division will give the writer a better grip and focus and help to divide the letters and words equally on the line. When pupils start to write their words and sentences too close or too far apart in the wide lined book, we will be able to remind them of the dot division.

The DVD
Learning to Write
This section of the DVD illustrates some of the areas identified in the text, including:
How to make a writing sheet
Drawing writing lines, 'boss and assistant'
Playing with (sound) words
Linking sounds
Creating animals.

Letters A to Z

Movement section

a

Basic movement: ocean wave / cats' noses

Loosening up to music: Track 2: Night
Track 13: Castle moat
Write Dance Track 8: Cats

Sound word section

Sound writing:

a   a   a   a   a   a   a   a   a

<u>a</u>   <u>t</u>   <u>a</u>   <u>t</u>   <u>a</u>   <u>t</u>   <u>a</u>   t   <u>a</u>

a   t   a   t   a   t   a   t   a

a   t   a   t   a   t   a   t   a

Join: sailing boat

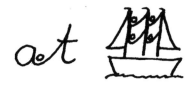

Write Drawing section

Pictorial letter: Anna

72

Playing with the letter

a

Anna: please refer to letters d and g.

Cats' noses (Ocean waves)

We are now looking at the three quarter rounded shape within the garland. We practised it in Write Dance. The brain will receive some feedback through motor skill practice accompanied by sounds. When our pencils or pieces of chalk (or fingers) have reached our noses, we say a loud 'meow' and put the drawing utensil down again. Then trace the drawing in different colours to consolidate and do not forget to finger dance on a dry and wet table board.

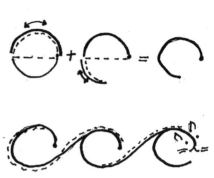

Anna and Okky (please refer to letter o)

An exercise that helps us to clearly distinguish the a from the o.

Letter a: A vertical down stroke with the rounded sailing boat join

Letter o: The horizontal good morning flick

Make a line of alternating a's and o's on nine dots. Consolidate the joins by tracing them and giving the Annas and Okkies different expressions. Anna always looks to the right and Okky looks straight ahead.

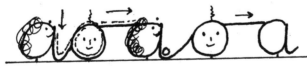

Open your mouth and close your mouth

Awareness of letters a remaining too open, which makes them look too much like c's or even like sharks' noses (please refer to letter c).

We make Anna sing.

Anna keeps her mouth shut.

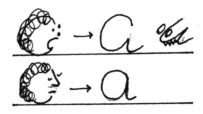

Movement section

b

Basic movement: Two looped garlands under each other

Loosening up to music: Track 8: Little Tea Ship
Track 16: Guests on Horseback
Write Dance Track 5: The Train

Sound word section

Sound writing:

b	b	b	b	b	b	b	b	b
<u>b</u>	<u>e</u>	<u>b</u>	e	<u>b</u>	e	<u>b</u>	e	<u>b</u>
b	e	b	e	b	e	b	e	b
b	e	b	e	b	e	b	e	b

Join: good morning

Write Drawing section

Pictorial letter: Rabbit b

Playing with the letter

b

Lawn (please refer to letters h, k, l)

Draw the looped grass letter symbol in different lengths and heights. Also draw short blades of grass and flowers.

Bibby and Crinklina are hiding in the grass.

Rabbit B

Draw the pictorial letter of Rabbit b with one ear. He is looking to the right.

Draw Rabbit b with two looped ears, looking straight ahead.

Soup spoon

The b is the only letter with an upper loop and a deep garland at the bottom. A soup spoon is a cute variation of the Little Tea Ship.

Mirror imaging: b and d (please refer to letters g, p and q)

We will do this on a table board or using sensorimotor materials.

1. Draw straight up and down strokes with both hands close together, switching to circles.

2. Make the d with the left hand, looking to the left and making the d sound.

3. Make the b with the right hand, looking to the right and making the b sound. Use another colour.

4. Move to the other side and discover the letters p and q.

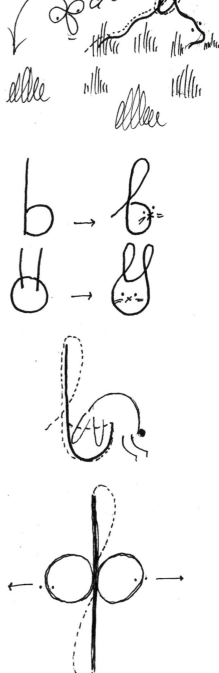

Movement section

Basic movement: ocean wave and cats' noses

CCccCcC C

Loosening up to music: Track 2: Night
    Track 13: Castle moat
    Write Dance Track 8: Cats

Sound writing:

c	c	c	c	c	c	c	c	c
<u>c</u>	<u>e</u>	<u>c</u>	<u>e</u>	<u>c</u>	<u>e</u>	<u>c</u>	e	<u>c</u>
c	e	c	e	c	e	c	e	c
c	e	c	e	c	e	c	e	c

Join: tea ship

Write Drawing section

Pictorial letter: Cats' nose

Playing with the letter

On the waves

There is also a round ocean wave in the letters a, d, g and q, but in the letter c we see it in its pure shape. Make a Write Drawing from ocean waves and draw a boat, a surfer and a wind surfer on top of the wave.

From the sea to the beach: The c, the p and the s

Make a drawing of yourself in an ocean wave and play in the surf. The ocean wave changes into a beach wave.

Make a series of ocean waves in slippy paint and see how they have become beach waves on the print.

Music: Ocean

This music is suitable for practising all kinds of different waves:

Calm weather: shallow waves

Light wind: small waves curling over

More wind: foam on the waves

Gale: whirlwinds and ocean waves

Sharks' noses

It is easier to make straight lines than round lines. Initially all children tend to apply short cuts to rounded shapes, which make shark's noses rather than a ocean waves. And of course the shark's nose is quite different to a cat's nose.

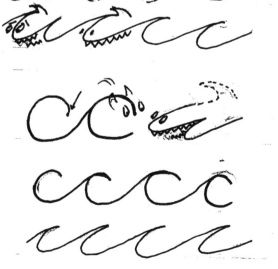

By practising the ocean waves and the cats' noses (please refer to letter a) we retain the upper curve that will make the bodies of the letters a, c, d, g and q recognisable.

Alternate a line of ocean waves and a line of sharks' noses to feel and see the difference. Add noises.

Movement section

d

Basic movement: . ocean wave and cats' noses

Loosening up to music: Track 2: Night
Track 13: Castle Moat
Write Dance Track 8: Cats

Sound word section

Sound writing:

d	d	d	d	d	d	d	d	d
<u>d</u>	<u>i</u>	<u>d</u>	<u>i</u>	<u>d</u>	<u>i</u>	<u>d</u>	i	<u>d</u>
d	i	d	i	d	i	d	i	d
d	i	d	i	d	i	d	i	d

Join: sailing boat

Write Drawing section

Pictorial letter: Anna balancing a stick on her nose

Playing with the letter

d

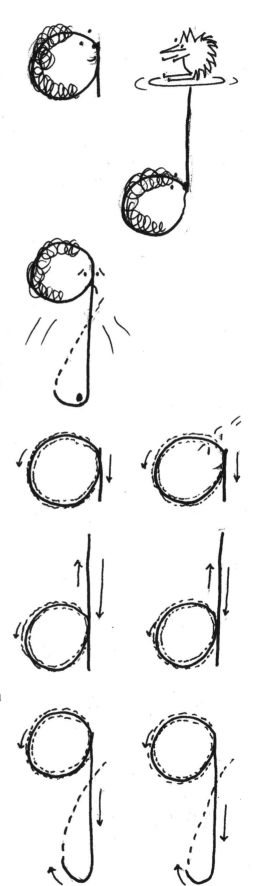

Anna is working in the circus: playing with the d, a and g

a: Anna is holding her hand in front of her face.

Just hold your own hand right in front of your nose, it is the down stroke of the a.

d: Anna is working in the circus and is balancing a stick on her nose.

Keep your arm stretched and close to your face and stick it up straight. Imagine it is a stick with a plate on top. Which cartoon figure do you recognise on the plate? Allow your arm to circle round a little.

g: Anna drops her stick. The plate with Hoggy, for example, falls on the ground. Quickly Anna catches the stick in her mouth. Keep your arm close to your mouth and bend over and let the stick (= your arm) dangle.

d, a and g: using sensorimotor skills and on the table board

a: Twist two hands to the left and say the a sound while you are doing so. Then suddenly say: 'Stop, Anna!' and make the downward stroke. Hold your hand in front of your face again.

d: Twist both hands to the left. Spluttering like a diesel engine you will say the d sound. While breathing in you draw the stick upwards and when breathing out forcefully you say: 'Do it Anna!' (or your own name..) and draw the downward stroke.

g: Circle round with both hands to the left, maybe while you are breathing in. When breathing out you draw a stick downward. At the bottom - on the left - you could draw some tiny circles if you like. Please refer to letter j: Music note.

Breathe in and take the loop back up again and imagine Anna placing the stick back on her nose.

First do these three exercises while finger dancing on a wet table board en then in chalk.

Movement section

e

Basic movement: looped garland

Loosening up to music:
Track 8: Little Tea ship
Track 25: Snowstorm
Track 16: Guests on Horseback
Write Dance Track 5: The Train

Sound word section

Sound writing:

e   e   e   e   e   e   e   e   e

e   l   e   l   e   l   e   l   e

e   l   e   l   e   l   e   l   e

e   l   e   l   e   l   e   l   e

Join: little tea ship

Write Drawing section

Pictorial letter: Eric

Playing with the letter

e

Crinklina - gallop

This exercise will make us conscious of the garland that stretches up to an upper loop.
To the 'horse music' in Dream Castle (the last theme) we first go round in circles on the spot. Crinklina is preparing herself for the race and is restless. Here we go: Garland loops to the left and to the right. Draw a couple of rows under each other. After 5-10 seconds the music is set to pause. Crinklina rears up. We draw a stick upward. When the music plays again, Crinklina gallops on and we complete the l-loop.

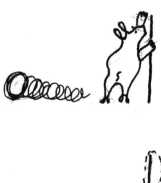

Eric drives in his car

We will express driving as we did the galloping in the previous exercise with garlands from left to right. As soon as Eric approaches a set of traffic lights, he looks up. This means we will draw an upper loop. If the traffic light is red, he will have to stop five counts, if it is green, he may drive on, if it is amber, he will drive slowly. This will be accompanied by engine noises.

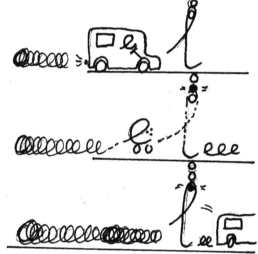

Concentration exercise: Sound writing and counting

This exercise needs nine dots in a row. We count out loud 1-2, 1-2-3, 1-2-3-4, and connect nine letters e in groups of two, three and four. Sounding the number should always coincide with the movement. Do this very slowly and note the synchronisation of sound and writing instrument.

Ele face

(Compare it with the ojo face in the letter j section)

Draw Eric with a long deep groove down his forehead.

Write draw the loops over it with and without preparatory turning movements to the left.

Movement section

f

Basic movement: standing eight or two looped garlands below each other

Loosening up to music: Track 18: Library
Track 29: Ice writing
Track 21: Bedroom
Write Dance Track 3: Circles and Eights

Sound word section

Sound writing:

f	f	f	f	f	f	f	f	f
f	a	f	a	f	a	f	a	f
f	a	f	a	f	a	f	a	f
f	a	f	a	f	a	f	a	f

Join: good morning

Write Drawing section

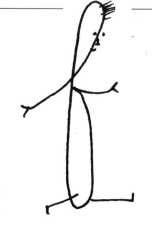

Pictorial letter: Freddy is doing his fitness exercises

Playing with the letter

f

f stretching himself or wide awake

We will make another Clover and lengthen the standing eight. The standing or awakening eight is now a foundation for the letter f. Freddy gets up at eight o'clock and stretches. Stretch your whole body - stretch your arms as high as you can.

Draw Freddy in the stretched loop.

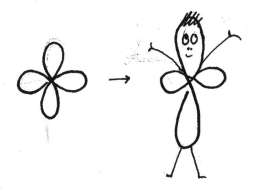

Loop-f

Draw a long, vertical line with a horizontal crossbar. The loops are hurrying towards us like a galloping Cinklina (please refer to the letter e) and stop when they reach the f's upper and lower loops.

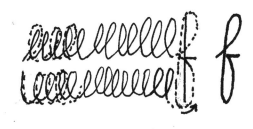

Garland-f and stretched eight-f can both occur in advanced writing. The double f, in particular, often occurs in stretched eights.

Freddy is doing his fitness exercises

Draw the upper half of Freddy's 'body' slightly to one side and then trace Freddy over it. Vary the position using different fitness postures.

The little men Sofos, Sefes and Safas

Three little men with an f-upper loop on their foreheads and an f-lower loop for their noses. They have s-ears and their eyes are in the vowels.

Write their names below.

Movement section

g

Basic movement: ocean wave and cats' noses and looped arches

Loosening up to music: Track 2: Night
Track 15: Entrance gate
Write Dance Track 8: Cats

Sound word section

Sound writing:

g   g   g   g   g   g   g   g   g

g   i   g   i   g   i   g   i   g

g   i   g   i   g   i   g   i   g

g   i   g   i   g   i   g   i   g

Join: lower loop

Write Drawing section

Pictorial letter: Anna drops her stick

84

Playing with the letter

g

Anna please refer to the letters a and d.

Full and narrow lower loop

Awareness of the lower loop:

We are standing up straight with the legs together. Now circle your writing hand over your stomach, to the left or to the right. This is the main body of the letter g. Slide one hand down your leg to your foot, because this is the stick of letter g. Draw the loop back up again via your other foot and leg.

Do this with your legs apart but also with your legs very close together.

Write Draw a number of figures with lower loops.

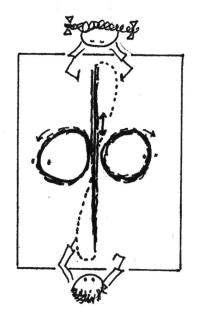

Exercise in mirror image: g and b (please refer to b, d, p, and q)

We will do this on a table board or using sensorimotor materials.

1. Make straight up and down strokes with both hands together, switching to circles.

2. Make the g with the left hand, looking to the left and making the g sound.

3. Make the b with the right hand, looking to the right and making the b sound. Use another colour.

4. Can you also trace the letters d and p?

Playing a game together: Catching circles (please also refer to letter p)

Pupil A draws a quick circle and pupil B quickly draws a stick through it or near it, wherever it happens to land. We will do this very quickly.

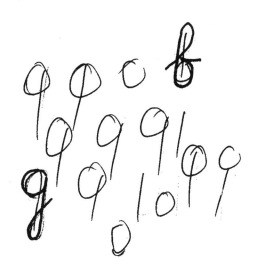

Check together which sticks have landed in the right places and that's where we draw the gs with a lower loop.

Take another colour to draw the bs.

Movement section

Basic movement: arch and upper loop

Loosening up to music: Track 3: Morning
Track 20: Basement (Mungojerry)
Track 15: Entrance gate

Sound word section

Sound writing:

h	h	h	h	h	h	h	h	h
<u>h</u>	<u>i</u>	<u>h</u>	<u>i</u>	<u>h</u>	<u>i</u>	<u>h</u>	<u>i</u>	<u>h</u>
h	i	h	i	h	i	h	i	h
h	i	h	i	h	i	h	i	h

Join: sailing boat

Write Drawing section

Pictorial letter: Harry

Playing with the letter

h

Lawn, loop exercise (please refer to letter b)

Narrow and wide arches

Write Draw Harry's sister Hihi and give her a pretty long skirt.

Please also refer to the exercises accompanying m and n.

Harry and Rodoggy

We can play the following game to assist our awareness of space between the letters:

One pupil represents Rodoggy, ties a skipping rope round the waist and crawls on hands and feet. Harry is the other pupil and will take Rodoggy out. Occasionally Rodoggy does not want to go and the line is taught, and next it will be slack.

Tie two skipping ropes together to make a very long line.

Then we Write Draw Harry and Rodoggy together with long and short joins.

In the sound word section you can skip a dot to experience extra width.

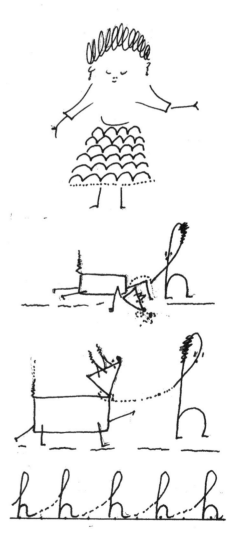

Movement section

Basic movement: sailing boat movement

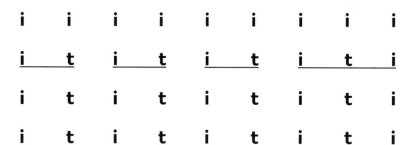

Loosening up to music: Track 1: Sailing Boat

Sound word section

Sound writing:

i	i	i	i	i	i	i	i	i
<u>i</u>	<u>t</u>	<u>i</u>	<u>t</u>	<u>i</u>	<u>t</u>	<u>i</u>	<u>t</u>	<u>i</u>
i	t	i	t	i	t	i	t	i
i	t	i	t	i	t	i	t	i

Join: sailing boat

Write Drawing section

Pictorial letter: The sailing boat

Playing with the letter

Music drawing The Sailing Boat

We will practise sailing boat connections to make the handwriting more resilient and we will play with the heights of the letters t and i. First do this on a table board.

No right angles

No round garlands

But the sailing boat join

A little circle will help to curve the corner.

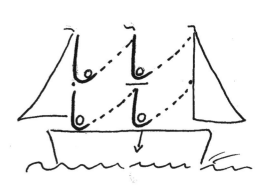

Sailing boat join

The sailing boat join will also be practised when connecting letters a d h l m n p r t u and it prevents developed handwriting from becoming too rounded or too straight. It is possible to make up interesting 'sound word sentences' with these 'sailing boat letters':

hadi mina turi.

Moving feet

After reciting the writing posture rhyme we will move our feet up and down as if balancing a ball on our feet.

Of course this will be easier in the PE hall where we can draw the letter i if there is a board available to show the relationship between the written and physical expression of movement.

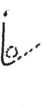

Please also refer to the letter t.

Movement section

Basic movement: looped arch

Loosening up to music: Track 15: Entrance gate
Track 20: Basement (Mungojerry)

Sound word section

Sound writing:

j   j   j   j   j   j   j   j   j

<u>j   o   j   o   j   o   j   o   j</u>

j   o   j   o   j   o   j   o   j

j   o   j   o   j   o   j   o   j

Join: lower loop

Write Drawing section

Pictorial letter: John

Playing with the letter

j

Swimming and diving

John is running the hurdle race

Music note

First draw music notes as support shapes. The little ball shows the direction of the lower loop.

Ojo and ele and Long Nose (please refer to letters e and l)

We will write ele in a continuous revolving movement to the left.

If we turn it round as if we are writing ele upside down, it will create Long Nose. The movement now continues to the right.

Practising ele and Long Nose is a good way of learning how to cross lines, for the distinction between upper and lower loops, and for the alternation of arches and garlands.

ojo is the sound word that resembles Long Nose most of all. ojo requires more advanced motor skills than Long Nose, because of the alternating left/right movements.

Divide the table board or paper into 16 fields and alternate writing ele Long Nose and ojo.

First give ojo and Long Nose a straight nose and then wind the loop around it. In the same way ele will first acquire a deep groove in his brow.

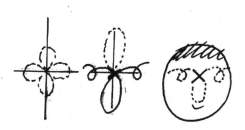

Movement section

Basic movement: sharp corners or ocean wave with an upper loop

Loosening up to music: Track 3: Morning
Track 9: Stepped Gable
Write Dance Track 4: Robot

Sound word section

Sound writing:

k   k   k   k   k   k   k   k   k

<u>k</u>   <u>e</u>   <u>k</u>   <u>e</u>   <u>k</u>   <u>e</u>   <u>k</u>   e   k

k   e   k   e   k   e   k   e   k

k   e   k   e   k   e   k   e   k

Join: sharp corner or rounded   

Write Drawing section

Pictorial letter: Keke

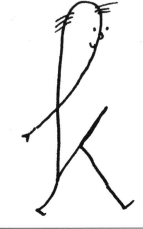

Playing with the letter

Kicking k and ocean k

The letter k is a difficult letter and often resembles letter h in advanced writing.

We can write this letter in two ways:

1 The kicking k grows out of pure sharp corners.

2 The ocean k is a softened simplification of the kicking k.

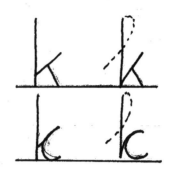

Lawn with Crickle and Hoggy and Rodoggy (straight cartoon figures)

Please also refer to letters b, h and l.

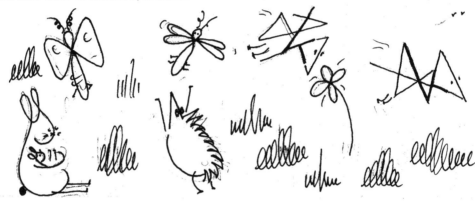

Small and big kicking k

First accompany the movement by counting to four, then to the music of Stepped Gable in Dream Castle. That is how we make the small k.

We will accompany capital K by counting up to three which will be easy to the music of the Roofs from Dream Castle.

Make a crinkle k animal with hard and 'sharp' sounds such as ki-ko-ka-ki.

Ocean k

First accompany the movements by counting to two, and then to music from Ocean.

Make a crinkle-k-animal with some gentler and 'rounder' sounds such as ca-li-do-go-co.

Movement section

Basic movement: looped garland

Loosening up to music: Track 8: Little Tea ship
Track 16: Guests on Horsebacks
Write Dance Track 5: The Train

Sound word section

Sound writing:

l l l l l l l l

l a l a l a l a l

l a l a l a l a l

l a l a l a l a l

Join: little tea ship

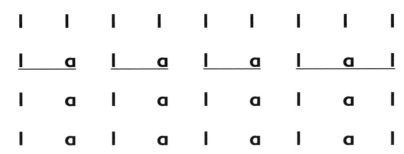

Write Drawing section

Pictorial letter: Loopy

Playing with the letter

Traffic light game (please refer to letter e)

First accompanied by engine noises, next by pieces of music of 5-10 seconds.

An anchor on the lawn

Little Tea Ship join

The joins of the l, e and c are round. We call it the little tea ship join and we can practise it with the music drawing of the same name. The join concerns the flat garland at the top of the Little Tea Ship. Also compare the flat or sleepy top of the letter r.

Face ele (please refer to letter e)

1. The letter l is a groove down the forehead.

2. First draw a circle to the left and then draw the looped groove across the forehead. This is in preparation of the word ele.

3. Draw more faces in which you write ele immediately.

4. Draw Long Noses (please refer to letter j).

5. Draw ojos and give some faces eye-masks.

Fold a sheet of paper and divide the table board into 16 squares. Continue to jump a square so that you can draw straight figures between them.

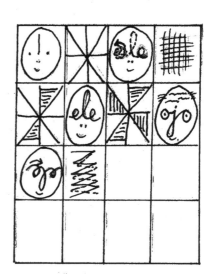

Movement section

Basic movement: arch without a loop

Loosening up to music: Track 3: Morning
                            Track 20: Basement (Mungojerry)
                            Track 15: Entrance gate
                            Write Dance Track 8: Cats

Sound word section

Sound writing:

m   m   m   m   m   m   m   m   m

<u>m</u>   <u>e</u>   <u>m</u>   <u>e</u>   <u>m</u>   <u>e</u>   <u>m</u>   e   <u>m</u>

m   e   m   e   m   e   m   e   m

m   e   m   e   m   e   m   e   m

Join: sailing boat

Write Drawing section

Pictorial letter: Monster

Playing with the letter

m

Me, you and the world

We write from left to right, from me to the other person. When writing letter n we move from our left legs to the other person's right leg. When writing the m we take it a step further.

Convert the number 10101 into a line of letters m with thick posts. Say: me - you - and the world

A crinkly animal hops across.

Focus on the 'me-post'

To ensuring that the m retains its stability we will trace over the ms' and ns' vertical me-posts a few extra times using number 10101, or 101.

Make the number 1 legs nice and sturdy by tracing up and down. The COS monkey (please refer to letter s) is jumping up and down on the posts and lets itself slide down. Make a nice sound to go with it.

Waddling arches

Arches 'waddling' to the left and to the right.

Waddle along while remaining upright!

Monster teeth

How many teeth will fit in the mouth of a monster?

Mumuphant

Ellybelly is given m-legs.

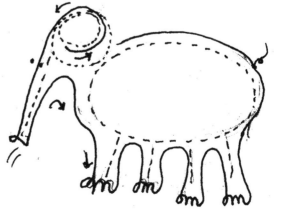

Movement section

Basic movement: arch without a loop

Loosening up to music: Track 3: Morning
Track 20: Basement (Mungojerry)
Track 15: Entrance Gate
Write Dance Track 8: Cats

Sound word section

Sound writing:

n	n	n	n	n	n	n	n	n
<u>n</u>	<u>u</u>	<u>n</u>	<u>u</u>	<u>n</u>	<u>u</u>	<u>n</u>	<u>u</u>	<u>n</u>
n	u	n	u	n	u	n	u	n
n	u	n	u	n	u	n	u	n

Join: sailing boat

Write Drawing section

Pictorial letter: Nina

Playing with the letter

n

Focus on the me-post (please refer to letter m)

Make a line of letters n out of number 101 with thick posts. Say: me and you.

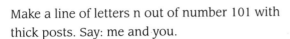

'Paint' the number-posts in different colours to draw attention to the me-post.

Tunnels

Breathe in: Draw an arch to the right or 'going there'

Breathe out: Draw an arch to the left or 'going back'

Nunu-nina

Crinklina is given n-legs. Trace the letters n in different colours.

Write the name nunu-nina under your drawing: a good sailing boat joining exercise. Please refer to letter i.

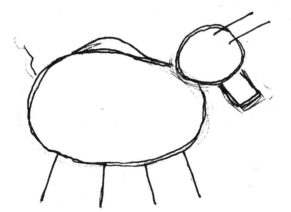

Movement section

o

Basic movement: looped garland

Loosening up to music:
Track 5: Whirlwinds
Track 25: Snowstorm
Track 16: Guests on Horseback
Write Dance Track 5: The Train

Sound word section

Sound writing:

o   o   o   o   o   o   o   o   o

<u>o</u>   t   <u>o</u>   t   <u>o</u>   t   <u>o</u>   t   <u>o</u>

o   t   o   t   o   t   o   t   o

o   t   o   t   o   t   o   t   o

Join: good morning

Write Drawing section

Pictorial letter: Okky

Playing with the letter

o

Good morning flick

We imagine when drawing this horizontal and straight join that we are greeting each other shaking hands or tapping our caps.

Depending on the next letter the join will turn slightly upward or downward.

Imagine a small child putting up its hand to greet the grown up and the grown-up bending down.

The straight good morning flick could be replaced by a loop in advanced handwriting.

Okky has got one aerial

The letter o begins and ends at the top, which is where Okky has one aerial right at the top of his head. He is a robot and Rodoggy is his friend.

Anna and Okky on one line (please refer to letter a)

Okky greets Anna with the horizontal join and his hand touching his cap.

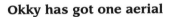

The a however, has a vertical stick downward and is joined to the following letter by means of a sailing boat join.

A stand

Okky and Anna are sitting on the stand of a football stadium. Please draw hundreds of faces.

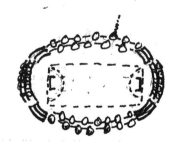

Snowman and snowballs

Drawing circles is something any child will enjoy.

The music from Snowstorm will help us make lots of snowmen and we will have a snowball fight.

Movement section

p

Basic movement: beach wave or arch without a loop

Loosening up to music: Track 6: Island
Track 26: The snow is settling
Write Dance Track 8: Cats

Sound word section

Sound writing:

p   p   p   p   p   p   p   p   p

p   e   p   e   p   e   p   e   p

p   e   p   e   p   e   p   e   p

p   e   p   e   p   e   p   e   p

Join: beach wave or sailing boat

Write Drawing section

Pictorial letter: Pepe

Playing with the letter

p

The letters a, c, d, g and q of the Cat family require us to slide our hands over our heads and when we touch our noses we will say 'meow'.

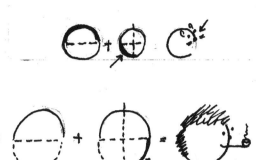

The following beach wave requires us to slide our hands from the back of our heads to our throats. We will grab a piece of skin and make different noises in our throats. The movements go sideways similar to those of cats' noses.

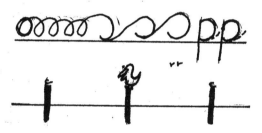

Two kinds of p:

1. Beach waves   p closed underneath

The beach wave emerges from the circle revolving clockwise and the arch.

Breakwaters are close to the beach and the waves come rolling in. First draw a row of posts across the line and then draw waves passing over them.

'Paint' the posts thickly in different colours to consolidate the movement as we did previously with the letters m and n.

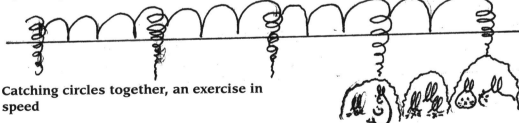

2. Bunny hop   p open underneath

Bibby has dug a number of rabbit burrows and is looking for his family. Vertical 'painting' will be replaced by circular digging movements.

Catching circles together, an exercise in speed

Please refer to letter g. Which letters can you turn into ps and which into gs?

Mirror imaging

Please refer to letters b and g.

Movement section

Basic movement: ocean wave / cats' noses

Loosening up to music: Track 10: Roofs
Track 22: Studio
Write Dance Track 4: Robot

Sound word section

Sound writing:

| q | q | q | q | q | q | q | q | q |

| q | e | q | e | q | e | q | e | q |

| q | e | q | e | q | e | q | e | q |

| q | e | q | e | q | e | q | e | q |

Join: sharp join

Write Drawing section

Pictorial letter: q-flower

Playing with the letter

q

Flower field / alpine meadow

The q is a suitable letter to be turned into flowers and mandalas. Place the q-flowers among the looped grass (please refer to letters l, h, b and k) and in a mountain meadow to have a sense of sharp corners.

We will practise the vertical down stroke and the sharp join to straight music.

Say: one - two - one - two and put a bit more pressure on the down stroke. First draw a couple of circles on the line.

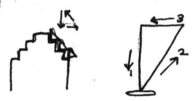

Flower vases

In Dream Castle we draw the roof tops with the point upward and count to three.

However, we practise the triangle with the point downward for the q-join. They are flower vases. Don't forget to count to three!

We will put flowers in the vase to the climbing roses music from Roofs.

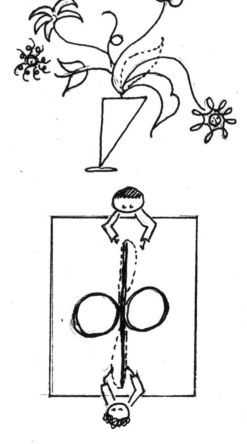

Mirror imaging (please refer to letter b)

Instead of letter q we can also use number 9 for 'mirror imaging'.

Movement section

Basic movement: garland without a loop

Loosening up to music: Track 8: Little Tea ship
Track 21: Bedroom
Write Dance Track 2: A Walk in the Country

Sound word section

Sound writing:

r	r	r	r	r	r	r	r	r
r	o	r	o	r	o	r	o	r
r	o	r	o	r	o	r	o	r
r	o	r	o	r	o	r	o	r

Join: sailing boat

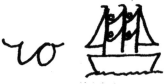

Write Drawing section

Pictorial letter: Sleepy Roro

Playing with the letter

r

Little Tea ship

This music is generally relaxing and can be used with many letters and joins: for the deep garland of the u, v and w (but also of the b), including the rather flat garland at the bottom of the c, e and l, and at the top of the r.

Two kinds of r:

1. The basketball-r

We will draw a sturdy post on the table board or on a big sheet of paper. 'Paint' it thickly in different colours. Please refer to letters m, n and p.

When we hear the first 'drops of water' of the music of the Little Tea Ship we draw the net.

Breathe in and have a good stretch.

Cast the ball into the net and sway along with the melody.

Draw the letter r along the net. We will also draw the ball and Anna and Okky, who are playing basketball.

2. The tap-r

Anna is thirsty and drinks from the tap.

This reading letter r is often used in advanced handwriting at the end of a word. It emerges from a semi-arch.

Roro is sleepy, Roro is awake

When Roro is asleep, we can tell by the shallow garlands that make up his eyes. When he is awake the deep u-garlands indicate his eyes are wide open.

Movement section

Basic movement: eights or beach waves

$$\text{ffff}\,\text{cccc}\,\text{S}$$

Loosening up to music: Track 17: Hall
Track 29: Ice writing
Write Dance Track 3: Circles and Eights

Sound word section

Sound writing:

s	s	s	s	s	s	s	s	s
<u>s</u>	<u>u</u>	<u>s</u>	<u>u</u>	<u>s</u>	<u>u</u>	<u>s</u>	<u>u</u>	<u>s</u>
s	u	s	u	s	u	s	u	s
s	u	s	u	s	u	s	u	s

Join: beach wave

Write Drawing section

Pictorial letter: Duckling s

108

Playing with the letter

Two kinds of s:

1. s-ducks are swimming on the line

First draw a row of standing eights on the line and
then trace the s-ducks over them.

s-duck has a stretch

Draw a row of stretched or wakeful eights (please
refer to letter f) over and under the line.

In the fairy tale the ugly duckling appears to be a
swan. We can turn the s-ducks into f-swans.

COS or Yin Yang-monkey

As we did for the little man Sofos with the letter f we
will draw a circle in a continuous movement with a
standing eight in it. The letters c, o and s merge into
each other. Occasionally lift your finger, piece of chalk
or pencil and continue moving it through the air. Of
course we will hum or sing along or draw to round
music.

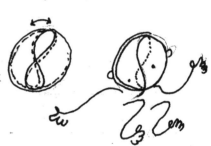

Walking eights

First trace a couple of eights over each other before
you join it to the next one. Experiment placing them
close to each other and further apart. Please refer to
letter h.

2. Surf-s

We leave a piece of the surf board emerging above
the wave to allow for the tight join of the letter s. It
indicates the flick on the letter s.

Please also refer to letter c. On the waves.

Movement section

Basic movement: sailing boat movement

Loosening up to music: Track 1: Sailing Boat

Sound word section

Sound writing:

t	t	t	t	t	t	t	t	t
t	e	t	e	t	e	t	e	t
t	e	t	e	t	e	t	e	t
t	e	t	e	t	e	t	e	t

Join: sailing boat or good morning

Write Drawing section

Pictorial letter: Ship's mast

Playing with the letter

t

Music drawing The Sailing Boat

The letters t and i emerge from the rounded garland corner which we practise in the music drawing the Sailing Boat.

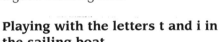

The t can be joined from the t-crossbar by means of a good morning flick.

Playing with the letters t and i in the sailing boat

Shooting off

1. Drawing quick straight lines is good practice for developing boldness and speed.

Place a couple of balls of paper on the table board and wipe them off with quick, confident lines of chalk.

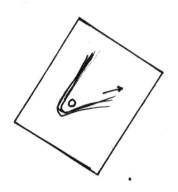

2. Place the balls in a row and draw big letters t and i around them or write another letter belonging to this sailing boat join. (a d h i m n r t u)

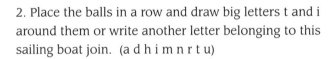

Hunting crosses

Player A quickly places a random vertical stroke and player B quickly tries to cross it. Which crosses can be turned into a t? If there is a clear difference in length you could also turn it into the letter f, which is based on a cross, too.

You can even hunt crosses with the letter x.

Movement section

u

Basic movement: garland without a loop

Loosening up to music: Track 8: Little Tea Ship
                                Track 13: Castle Moat

Sound word section

Sound writing:

u	u	u	u	u	u	u	u	u
<u>u</u>	**r**	<u>u</u>	**r**	<u>u</u>	**r**	<u>u</u>	**r**	<u>u</u>
u	r	u	r	u	r	u	r	u
u	r	u	r	u	r	u	r	u

Join: sailing boat

Write Drawing section

Pictorial letter: Uppy

112

Playing with the letter

u

Music drawing: The Little Tea Ship

This music drawing will help you find your own style and swing in deep or shallow (sleepy) round movements. Compare it with the letter r.

The letter u is a deep round one and wide awake.

The u has a sailing boat flick.

The v has a good morning flick.

Uppy has his legs up in the air

The letters u and n are acrobats and are somersaulting over the ground.

You could tilt the paper or move to the other side of the table board to discover the symmetry of the letters.

Please refer to the mirror exercise for the letters b, g, p and q.

Falling tea or autumn leaves

Keep the leaves 'wide awake', have them make deep swings from side to side and don't allow them to become 'sleepy' or shallow like in the letter r.

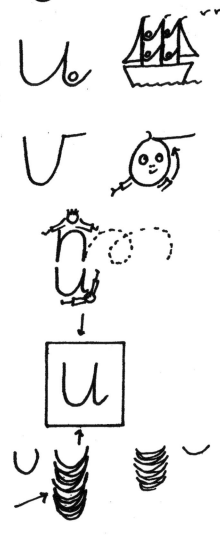

Movement section

Basic movement: sharp corners or garlands without loops

Loosening up to music: Track 8: Little Tea ship
Track 24: Snow crystals
Write Dance Track 4: Robot

Sound word section

Sound writing:

v   v   v   v   v   v   v   v   v

<u>v   a   v   a   v   a   v   a   v</u>

v   a   v   a   v   a   v   a   v

v   a   v   a   v   a   v   a   v

Join: good morning   

Write Drawing section

Pictorial letter: Master v

Playing with the letter

A line of sharp corners

In order to distinguish between the round u and the oval v we start with drawing mountain tops, first accompanied by counting, next to straight music.

We consolidate the ovals to round music.

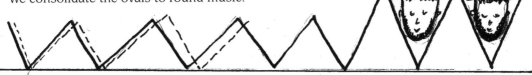

Good morning flick

Just like the letter o the v is joined with a horizontal flick. We greet each other by shaking hands or tapping our caps with our hands.

Master v with a beard and bow tie

By giving Master v a beard we emphasise the oval shape. Hold your hands in a v shape and rest your head in them.

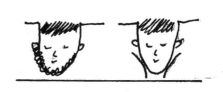

Put some shaving foam on your chin and scrape it off with a plastic spoon.

We give Master v a bow tie or a straight tie which reminds us of the hidden corner shape in the letter v.

Movement section

Basic movement: sharp corners or garlands without loops

Loosening up to music: Track 8: Little Tea ship
Track 24: Snow crystals
Write Dance Track 4: Robot

Sound word section

Sound writing:

w	w	w	w	w	w	w	w	w
<u>w</u>	o	<u>w</u>	o	<u>w</u>	o	<u>w</u>	o	<u>w</u>
w	o	w	o	w	o	w	o	w
w	o	w	o	w	o	w	o	w

Join: good morning

Write Drawing section

Pictorial letter: Master v's dog

116

Playing with the letter

Capital letter W

We draw a row of mountain tops or v shapes distinguishing between big and small or high and low. Have another try varying pressure.

We count to four while writing capital letter W, just like capital letters E and M. Please refer to Capital letters to straight and round music.

In pairs of two letters you can count to eight. This works well to the music of the Stepped Gable in Dream Castle.

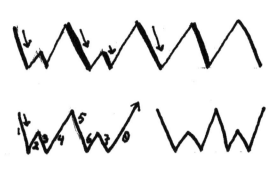

The small w

We will consolidate the w with the Little Tea Ship.

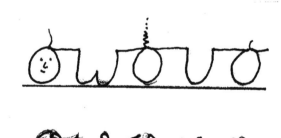

Good morning flick

Please refer to letters o and v. The straight good morning flick may turn into a loop in advanced handwriting.

Master v's dog

This is Rodoggy's robot friend. We will take him to the living animal world by making round movements.

Movement section

Basic movement: beach wave combined with ocean wave

Loosening up to music: Track 3: Morning
Track 27: Penguins
Write Dance Track 4: Robot

Sound word section

Sound writing:

x x x x x x x x x

<u>x i</u> <u>x i</u> <u>x i</u> <u>x i</u> <u>x</u>

x i x i x i x i x

x i x i x i x i x

Join: little tea ship

Write Drawing section

Pictorial letter: Fat tummies-x

118

Playing with the letter

The straight x as a support shape

The studio music in Starhome (Track 17) is highly suitable for making diagonal crosses.

First count slowly to two and think of variations at graded levels of difficulty. We use the straight x as a support shape and trace the round x over it.

Writing and dancing

-Cross-step: draw up your knees and touch them with your hands crossed in a nice swing.

-Cross-step dance: hold each other's hands and stretch your legs in alternation. Take three steps to the left and three steps to the right.

Chain-exercise

A repeat of write dancing: a good loosening up exercise for arches, garlands, eights and waves.

The round x: crashing waves

We will make round music beach waves and ocean waves.

Kolam, Indian art

1. Garlands with round music around six points.

2. Practise in four different directions.

3. Divide / fold table board or paper into 16 squares.

Give the four centre dots a different colour.

4. Make a kolam design out of four-leafed clovers.

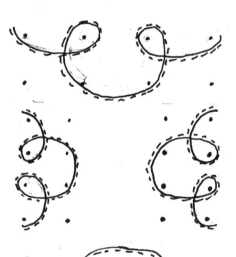

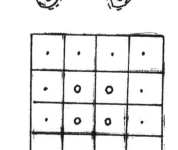

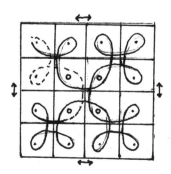

Movement section

Basic movement: garland without a loop and a looped arch

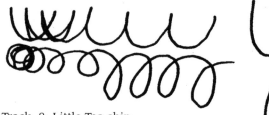

Loosening up to music: Track 8: Little Tea ship
Track 21: Bedroom
Track 15: Entrance Gate

Sound word section

Sound writing:

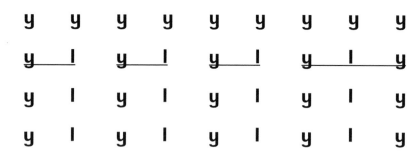

Join: lower loop

Write Drawing section

Pictorial letter: Mother and child

Playing with the letter

y

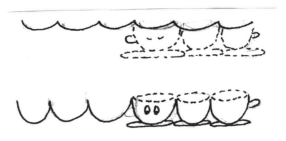

Garlands and arches

Swinging and swaying are relaxing movements. Left and right are given equal chances; emotions and experiences slip into the subconscious and are processed while sleeping.

First make a row of garlands to Little Tea Ship or any other round music.

Make a row of arches below to round music.

Finally trace the letter y over them.

Turning

Move across the table board or turn the paper upside down and you will be writing the letter h. Of course you will give it another colour and sound.

If y keeps its roots in the soil, h can become a big and beautiful tree.

Discovering letters

By playing with garlands and arches with and without loops we discover many letters.

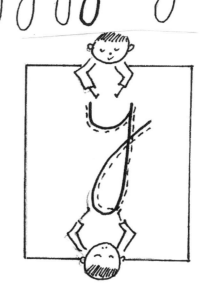

Movement section

Basic movement: sharp corners and waves

Loosening up to music: Track 10: Roofs
Write Dance Track 7: Silver Wings over the Sea

Sound word section

Sound writing:

z	z	z	z	z	z	z	z	z
z	e	z	e	z	e	z	e	z
z	e	z	e	z	e	z	e	z
z	e	z	e	z	e	z	e	z

Join: wave

Write Drawing section

Pictorial letter: Zig-zag

From a straight z to a wavy z:

Walking roofs

We will first trace a couple of roofs to the Roof music in Dream Castle, and then we make them walk like the walking eights (please refer to letter s). But of course first without music, counting slowly up to three.

Zig-zag

The zig-zags need to be arranged in a regular line.

Fluid waves

Play the Ocean or Silver Wings in Write Dance and trace several waves over each other.

Next we create beautiful rows.

Combine straight and round and discover the wavy letter z.

Robot swans and living swans

Straight movements can be associated with the Robot in Write Dance and are therefore also called 'robot movements'. They speak to the imaginative child in a better way than an abstract word such as 'straight'.

First we draw all kinds of robot swans accompanied by our voices and we consolidate them by tracing them to straight music.

We will bring them to life to Castle Moat music and we will have them swim in the castle moat around the castle.

Capital letters accompanied by straight and round music

A considerable number of capitals have a basic structure which we can draw to the rhythm of 'straight' music. We will count out loud.

Certain capitals, such as the V, consist of two straight lines; other capitals, such as the F, consist of three straight lines. There are a few more, for example the E, which consist of four straight lines.

The musical criterion - should we count in twos, threes or fours - presents us with a new way of learning the foundation of 'straight' capitals. Round versions of the same capitals can be traced over the straight support shapes.

It leaves us with two other categories of capitals: letters such at the O which are completely round, or the capitals such as the B that incorporate the straight as well as the round shapes. It is possible to learn those to music, too.

Capitals while counting (straight)

Practical method

Consolidating the basic structure

> The teacher will write the 'straight' version of one or two letters in the same group on the board in big letters, e.g. the one-two-group. While facing away from the class the teacher will demonstrate the movements in the air. The pupils copy, first counting, then to music.

> Next the children continue the movements on a writing surface counting out loud to music.

Applying curves

> Play some 'round' music: The pupils will now trace round shapes in other colours over the capitals according to their own ideas or according to the example the teacher has written on the board.

Music suggestion for 'round' music:

Track 13: Castle Moat
Track 29: Ice writing
Track 21: Bedroom
Track 26: The snow is settling

Count out loud: one - two   V   L   Y   X   T

Music suggestion

Track 4: Robot   Track 22: Studio
Track 12: Brickwork   Track 24: Snow crystals

Count out loud: one - two - three K   A   F   N   Z   H   I

Music suggestion

Track 10: Roofs
Track 22: Studio

Count out loud: one - two - three - four   W   E   M

Music suggestion

Track 9: Stepped gable
Track 28: Breaking Ice

Capitals *round*   C   O   S

Write these letters following each other, but also in one continuous line and create a monkey!

Music suggestion

Track 13: Castle Moat   Track 29: Ice writing
Track 21: Bedroom   Track 26: The snow is settling

Capitals *straight / round*   B   D   G   J   P   Q   R

Write these letters following each other on the board or on a big sheet of paper:

BDGJ PQR

First trace and consolidate the straight line parts of these letters while you say:

'Straight. Straight. Straight.'

BDGJ PQR

Next trace and consolidate all the round lines while you say: 'Round. Round. Round'.

Additional remarks

- Don't forget to finger dance.

- Write sound words such as KALIMO or BUDERA in capitals. This can also be done on the writing surface or in a wide-lined book.

- When the capitals in question have been consolidated the pupils can 'frame' the 'capitals' and/or decorate the edge of the paper, while the music is still playing.

- Write your own name with a capital at the beginning. Turn the initial letter into a fully decorated initial, like medieval monks did.

Numbers accompanied by straight and round music

We can distinguish straight lines and curves in numbers as we do in capital letters. Put them together in groups, count out loud or play some round and straight music.

In Write Dance in the Mandala we did a finger exercise with numbers. We will repeat that exercise in preparation: In each group we will say the numbers and spread a matching number of fingers.

Straight numbers   1   4   7

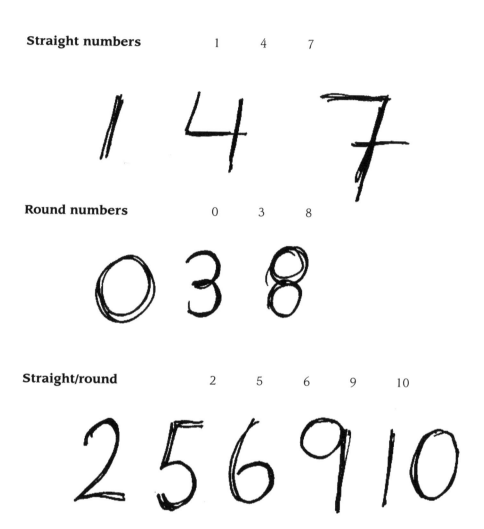

Round numbers   0   3   8

Straight/round   2   5   6   9   10

Chapter Four

Music Drawings

Writing means movements, movements require music. Therefore Write Dance uses music as a motor to start up the handwriting. Musical accompaniment creates a natural balance between tension and relaxation. It applies to all children, but most of all for whom learning to write is a slow and hard process. Melody and rhythm are wholesome and restorative. Writing movements to music increase resilience and elasticity, and the results will be apparent in body language and handwriting. The music pieces which have been referred to in the alphabetical part of the previous chapter, will reappear in this section as the building blocks for six music drawings, which might be a compilation of several music tracks and Write Drawings.

The principle of the music drawings is the same as it was in Write Dance. It always is an experience linked to a certain representation which will first be expressed by the whole body and then on a writing surface.

The music drawings have not been graded according to levels of difficulty: they can be completed in random order.

We will first practise the themes without music

It does not matter if we practise the movements whole body or on a writing surface, but it is important to plan them first without any music. It will enable us to work at our own pace initially, which we will mark by making our own sounds or counting aloud. We will always begin with movements, to be continued on a board or on paper. We first use our finger on the writing surface and change to chalk later. When it goes well we will play the music. If it is difficult to keep up with the music while we are Write Drawing we just lift our hands off the writing surface for a second without stopping our movements.

Finger dancing

A completed music drawing enables us to play music at any time during the week and finger dance on the table without losing time securing sheets of paper and yet consolidating the movements.

Splitting large music drawings

Dream Castle, Starhome and Snow consist of numerous short themes. It would be better to spread the themes over two or three lessons. We can put the sheets of paper away and continue next time.

Movement and shape

Children who like movement will enjoy creative expression, while children who enjoy shapes will want to see pretty results and tend to be a little less spontaneous.

The 'perfect' result would be a good balance between shape and movement (and space division). Some children appear not to hear the music while they are carrying out the themes. It does not really matter, because the music is still the motor and driving source that sparks off movement and creativity.

Exercises on lines

Each music drawing is completed with exercises on lines, which makes a good transition to handwriting. When the pupils are ready for exercises on lines, please use a folded writing sheet or a copied sheet from the CD-ROM, or give the children a wide-lined book to 'write' in. Of course we will first practise without music, while finger dancing, and then to music, tracing with different colour crayons or, if the pupils are ready, with a fountain pen.

Presentation of the music drawings

Hang a couple of home-made table boards on the wall or from the climbing frames, lay wallpaper rolls on the floor, use materials for dressing up, some face-paints and we are ready to perform the music "whole body" as well as on the board and paper.

The DVD

After reading the instructions on each of the six 'music drawings', watch the appropriate track on the DVD.

This should clarify the activities and help you to modify the instructions to suit the needs of your children.

Sailing Boat   CD Track 1

The well-known melody of Vangelis which he composed in 1992 for the film Columbus is easy to sing to. The title of this music drawing could have been 'Columbus', too. However, this Sailing Boat will allow us to sail across all the seas in the following music drawing Ocean Journey and it does not necessarily take us to America!

The Sailing Boat helps us to practise the garland corner or rounded corner of the Sailing Boat flick. But even without its specific purpose this music drawing is a good rhythmical exercise.

To achieve a better grip on the movements we will first make a drawing of the Sailing Boat.

Drawing the Sailing Boat

The teacher will draw a rectangle on the board and show how a big sheet of paper or a table board can be divided into sixteen squares by marking the middle at the side. A sheet of paper can also be folded into sixteen squares. Secure the paper or table board so that we can work with two hands, and then we will draw the Sailing Boat in five steps.

Boat

Three masts

Mainsail and jib

Crossbars

Rigging and circles

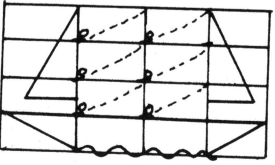

Whole body

Rowing

We sit at our own tables or in a line behind each other on the floor. Our legs are stretched. We are sitting in a rowing boat and rowing toward the big Sailing Boat.

During the introductory sequence we can imagine the solar rays playing on the waves and we illustrate this by shaking our fingers, hands and wrists in a slow fluttering movement. Try closing your eyes and feel the heat of the solar rays on your face.

The rowing theme begins with rhythmic percussion. The teacher stands arms stretched facing the group and counts along quietly. This takes a little getting used to. At an appropriate moment the teacher counts out loud and the children copy the teacher:

One *(tension)*: Pull your arms back and let your body lean back slightly. The rowing boat is big and heavy due to its load. Pull as hard as you can, leaning slightly backwards. It is not easy grasping the rowing rhythm straight away, many children find it difficult but it is a good rhythmical listening and moving exercise.

Two - three *(relaxation)*: We bring our arms and bodies back to the starting position and on the count of one we pull hard but slowly on the oars again. Let the children count along.

1 = towards you   2/3 = away from you

We repeat the rowing movements several times. After some training we will soon begin to feel the rowing rhythm in our bodies and arms. At first it might feel more logical to bend forwards on the first count, but then we will be out of sync with the downstrokes of our music drawings later on. Try to get into a regular, slow 'swing and waltz' rhythm.

Meanwhile, we have reached the large sailing vessel in our rowing boats and we climb aboard. Make rapid climbing movements with your hands and immediately start pulling the ropes to hoist the sails.

Hoisting the sails

On every first count we 'grab hold' of a big piece of rope in the air and on every second and third count we let our hands go up diagonally to the right creating a garland-corner. We could imagine a man pulling the rope and passing it on, or it could be sails that are flapping in the wind. The personal swing and style start from a feeling of tension and relaxation and again we try to carry out the exercise as rhythmically as possible, rocking along to the music. Instead of one - two / three we will now say; down - up, down - up in the same rhythm.

On the board and on paper

We see and feel sparkling sunny vibrations in the air, which we express with our hands. After that we make some garland-corner or rope pull-movements, first with our fingers only over the sailing boat drawing. We will take good note of the curves around the circles.

Next we will use the pieces of chalk while we continue to say down - up or one - two / three. Six sails are being hoisted. In spite of the circles it is not unusual for children to draw sharp corners initially instead of rounded corners. The teacher should continue to pay attention to this.

Sharp corners are not allowed

Garlands are not allowed

Garland-v-shapes should be produced

The foresail and the mainsail consist of real v-shapes. You can occasionally draw them to feel the difference compared with the garland-v-shape.

Water

The water hits the bow with great force. Whack! Make stretched movements or draw lines on the bow and water around the ship or simply enjoy your liberating movements in the air. (Sailing boat joins can be seen on the DVD.)

Hoisting the sails

Letter flicks (down and up)

Writing and counting

ha hi tina

Ocean Journey

The Ocean Journey is a good successor to the Sailing Boat, because its music takes us on an adventure! We can sail all the seas and go ashore anywhere we like. Where will the wind and the waves take us? The music is atmospheric and continues virtually uninterrupted. Unlike Dream Castle, Starhome and Snow the themes do not require specific movements. The music speaks to our feelings and inspires us to create lively representations with bodily expressions in the classroom, hall or on board and on paper.

Once again, use a large sheet of paper or board or shaving foam and blue slippy paint. The big surface represents the sea. On paper we can draw an island somewhere in the sea. During the first notes of the music we hear the voice of the teacher, narrator or assistant painting the atmosphere with a few words and inspiring the pupils to express themselves on the writing surface. The narrator's role could also be taken over by a pupil. Here are some suggestions:

Night   CD Track 2

It's night and we are quietly leaving the bay or the harbour. The sea is calm and a few stars are twinkling in the sky.

Morning   CD Track 3

The sun rises early like a big ball and we can hear the seagulls or cormorants screeching. The ropes are hoisted once more and the compass shows us the route.

Fishing boat   CD Track 4

A fishing boat catches up with us and we wave at each other. 'Have you caught plenty of fish?' We feel the waves gradually getting bigger. Up and down we bob, rolling from starboard to port... Then the skies are darkening in the distance. Suddenly the wind drops, we listen... is there a storm brewing?

Whirlwinds   CD Track 5

Yes, the wind is getting stronger and the weather is turning. Lower the sails, tie everything down! Here comes the first whirlwind. It is taking my cap! The ship is buffeted by the wind!

Island

Fortunately, the storm has died down and we realise that we are sailing past a beautiful island with flowers, butterflies, birds and... seals. We sail past and see a long shoreline in the distance. We are getting nearer. What is that moving on the beach?

Party

We have landed. The local people show us their dance. Perhaps we could decorate our drawings with small dashes round the edges? Or let the upper half of our body dance while we are sitting? If there is enough room, we will dance around the tables!

Night

Morning

Fishing boat

Whirlwinds

Island

Party

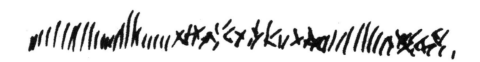

Little Tea Ship

The old Dutch song 'Schuitje varen, theetje drinken' (rough translation: "Going boating, drinking tea") is a nursery rhyme which will now after more than 100 years cross the Channel with Write Dance! Our new English text is as follows:

Little man in his rowing boat
Trying so hard to keep afloat
Bobbing up and bobbing down
Making sure he cannot drown
Merry little sailor

This also explains why we create 'teacups' in the Dutch garland exercises. Undoubtedly non-Dutch Write Dancers will also enjoy creating chains of teacups. We can imagine our merry little sailor feeling terribly cold, desperate for his old-fashioned flask of hot tea. Alternatively, maybe his rowing boat looked like a teacup. Perhaps he had painted it like a teacup, or perhaps he saw lots of cups and saucers floating past with wriggly worms inside. There are endless possibilities for children and teachers to let their imagination run riot with Write Dance!

Little Tea Ship is a short exercise that assists you giving curves in letters a rhythm of their own. The movements can be prepared "whole body" or just above the board or paper.

Whole body

The Little Tea Ship melody begins with xylophone sounds. We flick our fingers, from index to little finger when the melody starts on. We make rowing movements as we did with the Sailing Boat, or alternatively we draw big tea cups whole body.

On the board and on paper

We draw big rocking movements and will eventually draw masts and sails in them. That is how it becomes a real Little Tea Ship. If you like, you can draw a saucer underneath.

Dream Castle

This music drawing consists of eight themes which can be spread out over two or three lessons. All the themes are identified on the DVD.

1. Stepped Gable

CD Track 9

Whole body

Start slowly and without any music: the arms in the starting position are stretched out level with our heads. We hear four preliminary drumbeats. On the eight counts of trumpet notes (count out loud) we make seven slow downward movements with both hands in horizontal position. On the eighth count the arms are lowered all the way down to the desk or even to the ground (bend your knees!) Repeat four times.

We could turn our wrists at every descending gable step alternately in a horizontal and a vertical position to make it a little more difficult. (Practise this slowly and at first without music.) Simultaneously lower the arms gradually to the beat of the music.

On the board and on paper

The teacher begins to draw the movements on the board very slowly while counting aloud. The children do the same and count out loud, first only with their fingers on the paper or on the board. Instead of saying 'eight' when they reach the last count, they could also say 'down' to indicate that they have reached the steep wall.

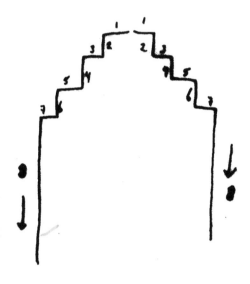

Repeat the movements a couple of times in chalk while standing or sitting behind the table, first slowly without music. Speed up the counting and then try with music. All the children are counting along.

2. Roofs and climbing roses

CD Track 10

Whole body

Roofs

After two counts to the beat the teacher counts to three and we form triangles with our arms representing the roofs on the battlements of the castle. The easiest and most logical method is starting from the centre drawing outward and from the top. Stay where you are at your desks or in your space. Later we can try to curtsey at each first count. After some practice we could do three steps forward and three steps back as a dance exercise.

Intermediate theme (CD 0:16)

Shake your body lightly when you feel the first vibration. This should be repeated three times. Sitting at our desks we give our wrists a quick shake to loosen them up.

Climbing roses (CD 0:47)

The whole body, including wrists and fingers, make circular climbing and twisting movements upwards and in different directions. Stay where you are while doing this.

On the board and on paper

Roofs

Trace each triangle twice. If you can't manage with both hands (difficult!), use the writing hand. Once again, first practise without any music and count aloud to three.

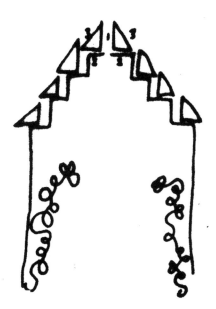

Intermediate theme (CD 0:16)

Give wrists and shoulder a little shake just above the table while holding the pieces of chalk.

Climbing roses (CD 0:47)

Make small, spiralling movements on either side of the castle wall using one or two hands. Then draw a flowerpot and decorate the flowers.

3. Bouncing Ball

CD Track 11

Whole body

Imagine that we are playing with a ball in the castle gardens and that the ball has ended up on the roof. On the final notes it spins round on the balcony.

Arms stretched wide, wrists turning round whilst lowering the arms.

On the board and on paper

Let the ball bounce downward in curves and spin round on the balcony, i.e. two horizontal lines on either side of the castle.

4. Brickwork

CD Track 12

Whole body

Draw dots or dashes in your space representing brickwork while sitting at your desk.

Alternatively, imagine we are on the balcony bouncing a ball. Bend the wrists, alternating left and right. When we hear the flute and the triangle (CD 0:16) we start throwing the ball towards each other. This makes an excellent PE exercise, with or without a ball.

On the board and on paper

Draw dots or dashes on the castle battlements.

When listening to the CD (starting at 0:16) we will connect all the dots with wriggly lines.

5. Castle Moat

CD Track 13

Whole body

Waltzing on the spot with our arms and our whole bodies, or as to be seen on the DVD, linking arms.

On the board and on paper

Make undulating movements with one or two hands. Show the water's different movements: 'waving or walking eights', ocean or beach waves. All are allowed and anything is acceptable, so long as the movements flow well.

6. Windows and staircase

CD Track 14

Whole body

March on the spot or draw large squares in the air. We are expecting guests. The windows have to be cleaned, the beds must be aired. Can we hear the guests approaching? While listening to the CD we climb the stairs, and perhaps carry trays and plates upstairs via the cellar stairs (CD 0:44). On the CD we can also hear someone dashing downstairs (CD 0:48).

On the board and on paper

Draw windows, with shutters if you like, to the beat of the music. Listening to the CD we will draw the staircase but it doesn't matter if it has passed before you realise!

7. Entrance gate

CD Track 15

Whole body

Wave your arms from side to side, just like we did in Cats in Write Dance, but this time make sure the arcade goes down to the ground. During the CD we will decorate the gate with garlands and flags. We make small loop movements with our wrists creating the same wide arch.

On the board and on paper

Draw a big arch as an entrance gate and some looped small arches decorated with garlands. The garlands could also frame the windows.

8. Guests on horseback

CD Track 16

Whole body

We now blow our trumpets, because our guests have arrived! Hold your fist in front of your mouth and make trumpet sounds to the left and to the right, moving your fist slightly up and down and stretching your arms.

As can be seen on the DVD, we can use the skipping ropes in the PE hall as bridles. Tell the children about farmers, noblemen and the way horses trot. We sit upright, greet our guests courteously or bounce up and down on a workhorse. If the class threatens to become too energetic we could slowly turn down the volume and finish off by skipping on our toes without music. Sitting at our desks we rotate our arms.

On the board and on paper

Holding a crayon in both hands, make trumpet movements in the air, stretching your arm while quickly drawing tight zigzags on top of each other each other at the sides of the castle. Draw loops round the music drawing to frame it. The horses and guests first gallop round the park. If there are too many, continue in the air just above the paper.

Castle Dance in the PE hall (Please refer to the DVD)

Attach two or three boards to the climbing frames so that the children can use them in alternation.

1. **Stepped gable:** The children stand in two lines facing each other. With our hands and arms we make seven step gables and a long wall downward. Bend your knees.

2. **Roofs:** Three steps forward, and three steps back. The girls curtsey, the boys bow.

   Additional theme: The boys nod and the girls shake their heads. When we hear the final 'balcony notes' the girls emphasise their 'no' with definite horizontal arm movements. 'No, no!'

   Climbing roses: The boys and girls link arms and dance slowly round the room.

3. **Bouncing ball:** We make four wide arch movements with our arms (maybe singing 'la-la-la-la....'), followed by round wrist movements, anti-clockwise or clockwise.

4. **Brickwork:** Mime bouncing ball movements or use a real ball, first without music. All that bouncing noise may almost drown the music.

5. **Castle moat:** The lines of boys and girls link arms and make swaying movements. This may create plenty of involuntary movements because lack of co-ordination tends to end in giggles!

6. **Windows and staircase:** The pupils stand facing each other. First we make the windows (don't forget to bend your knees) and clean them if they are dirty. Alternatively, march on the spot while waving the arms. When we hear the 'staircase' music we could march round the room or over a bench.

7. **Entrance gate:** Use ribbons made out of crepe paper or scarves. We make big movements to create the entrance gate, using our whole bodies and using our wrists to show the decorations (arcades and garlands) using the wrists.

8. **Guests on horseback:** Blow the trumpets in all directions. Play 'giddy-up' using skipping ropes.

Castle structure

Roofs

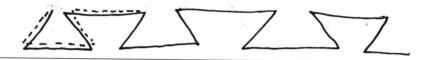

Climbing roses

Bouncing ball

Brickwork

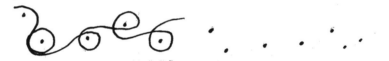

Castle moat

Windows and staircase

Entrance gate

Guests on horseback

Starhome

In Starhome we enter the house of a film or pop star where everything is beautiful and luxurious.

Maybe the artist has bought the Dream Castle. In each room we are introduced to a new set of movements and new ideas. In order to make it more exciting we will ask the children after having completed each theme to guess which room we will be moving into next.

Spread the six themes over two or three sessions. All the themes are identified on the CD.

1. Hall
CD Track 17

Whole body

We are now in a large entrance hall and we are amazed by its beauty. We walk around very slowly and admire the beautiful crystal chandelier, the paintings, the statues, the impressive balustrade, the designs on the tiles on the wall and the floor... What else can you see in such a big hall?

While sitting at the table, we only move our arms.

On the board and on paper

We can't draw everything we have experienced in such a short time. That's why we will choose a tile design so that we can add a writing motor skill aspect to the movements. We will create flowing and wavy horizontal and vertical lines based on the slow mysterious music.

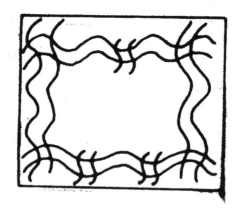

Without any music we will draw decorations around the edges of our boards or paper and ask the children to talk about them.

2. Library
CD Track 18

Whole body or sitting at the table

There is a nice open fire in the library. Listening to the first slow tune, we try to extinguish the tongue-like flames with our arms. The teacher may say out loud 'in-and-out-and- 'to indicate the tempo.

When we hear the second and faster tune we draw garlands alternated by downward strokes to show they are books. While doing so we count out loud: 'one (and a) two (and a) one (and a) two'. First practise this slowly without music.

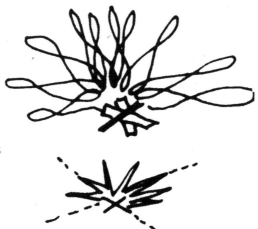

On the board and on paper

Open fire

The woodblocks are creating flickering flames in all directions but don't draw too fast. Try the movements with your pen and pencil just above the paper. Very often the flames become mere lines, while this exercise consists of looped movements. Give an example on the big board.

Bookcase

CD (1:21). We are going to draw big and small books made of garlands and downward strokes. Once again we will draw dashes for the 'titles and authors'. The teacher will count in a two or four-time beat for the respective slow and fast garlands.

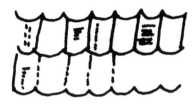

3. Kitchen (Dropping Ingredients)

CD Track 19

Whole body

Pans

With our arms and hands we pretend to be pans, cups, glasses, wooden spoons, etc. Maybe with a little help you can also rock from side to side on your back while holding your arms tightly round your knees. You have become a round dish or pan! The teacher assistant and pupil can do this together.

Sprinkling

Use your fingers to sprinkle herbs, sugar and salt into the pan, dropping your arms slowly downward. Stir everything in the pan. Also stir in the shape of a horizontal eight, which helps to mix everything well!

Steam

It is bubbling and boiling. Shake your whole body and stretch your arms when you hear the steam. While sitting at the table, we only move our arms.

On the board and on paper

Pans

Make dish-like movements backwards and forwards. You can draw pans, cups, mugs and glasses without lifting the chalk from the board.

Draw arches to turn the cups and pans upside down.

Sprinkling

Of course we will use dots or dashes to let our ingredients fall on our drawings. Encourage

the children to draw dashes, which is a bit more difficult. In a large group you can still hear the music with the dash rhythm. Making dots, however, will make more noise. Turn it into a counting game: four dashes on paper, and then bend your wrists four times just above the paper (holding the chalk). Finally stir in the shape of a spiral, to the right and to the left.

Steam

It is bubbling and boiling! We make quick movements from side to side without moving away and then quickly upwards. Stretch your arm up into the air and produce the sound of steam.

4. Basement

CD Track 20

Whole body

The stairs and the ghost

We can make a stairway with our hands just as we did in Dreamcastle . The music is quite fast, so only make the stairs with your hand held horizontally. Make flowing movements with your hands when you hear the immediately following melodious theme. Shall we also ask the children to play ghosts...?

Mungojerry

Wave your hands from side-to-side making arches or garlands or pretend you are a cat ready to jump. While sitting at the table, your hands show the steps and your arms show the melody.

On the board and on paper

Stairs

First draw a staircase without any music and with only one piece of chalk; we will walk up and down to the music as best we can! The next tune invites us to draw smooth joins. Now we will draw the ghost.

Mungojerry

There is a cat sneaking around, a bat flapping its wings, a hanging spider's web, a mouse shooting off.... This kind of music leads to many exciting experiences. First allow the children to express their feelings in drawings without music. Then the teacher draws a spider's web on the board which is woven in garlands, first without and then with music. The cat and mouse emerge from the same round arch.

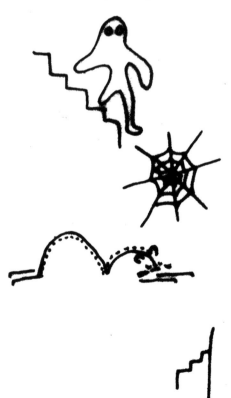

Now we are going to draw a secret stairway (or a revolving cupboard) without music in one of the corners of the basement. It leads to the bedroom.

5. Bedroom

CD Track 21

Whole body

This clearly is a rocking melody, which you can express in many different ways. For instance, with accompaniment (please refer to the pans), lying on your back, while you are swinging from side to side with your arms wrapped around you. Imagine you are lying in a hammock, or in a rocking cradle. While sitting at the table you only need to give your hands or body a quick wriggle.

On the board and on paper

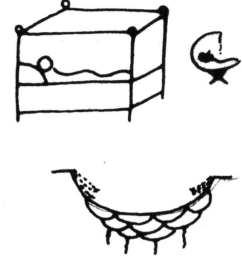

We could first draw the basic shape of a four-poster bed without music (give an example on the board). Decorate it with all kinds of variations with or without music. The cradle and the hammock are quite suitable for this theme, too. The cradle swings higher and higher in the shape of a c. The hammock is given some real Mexican plaiting. All the movements in the bedroom are round. In the next room, the studio, all the movements are straight.

6. Studio

CD Track 22

Whole body

This musical and film from the Eighties starts off with a line of dancers stretching their legs sideways in turn. Each child will first do so individually, then in pairs and finally the whole line. Do you think they will manage? While sitting at the table we stretch and bend our fingers and arms to the tempo of the music.

On the board and on paper

Single lines become crosses just like our legs. But first the children would like to draw the cameras, the stage, the spotlights... Ask them to draw everything in straight lines. Decorate the edge and draw zigzags.

Hall

Open fire

Bookcase

Kitchen

Basement

Bedroom

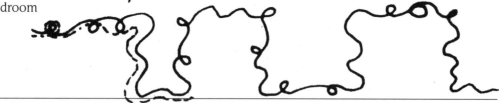

Studio

Snow

It is beginning to snow and it is growing very cold. Is it nearly Christmas? All the water is freezing up; maybe this will also happen to the ocean where the Sailing Boat and the Little Tea Ship are sailing...?

1. It is snowing!

CD Track 23

Whole body

We are standing in a circle or in a line and we stretch out our arms each time we hear the trumpeters. It is Christmas and with two arms we press down the branches of the Christmas tree by making semi-circular movements outwards and inwards.

We repeat the same movements while sitting at the table. You might say out loud: out-in-out-in.

On the board and on paper

We draw the sparkles at the top of the Christmas tree to the sound of trumpets. Then we draw the Christmas tree with two pieces of chalk, or with our hands with shaving cream or paint. Many children tend to draw the branches like triangles; therefore we need to encourage them to draw semi-circles to increase suppleness. First design the Christmas tree slowly without music by finger dancing to get the feel of round shapes. Next use some chalk or a sponge. Draw candles and garlands in the tree.

2. Snow crystals and stars

CD Track 24

Whole body

Stand somewhere in the hall and flick your fingers one by one or pick the stars from the sky. Occasionally turn your wrists inward and outward to the rhythm of the music. Draw up your legs in turn and bend your knees occasionally.

On the board and on paper

We flick away the shaving cream representing snow with our fingers. Then we draw big crosses, stars or snow crystals in it. The older children can give their imagination a free range on paper and try all kinds of variations.

3. Snowstorm

CD Track 25

Whole body

We turn around or stand still and only turn our wrists and arms. Little balls of paper are ideal for a snowball fight.

On the board and on paper

This theme invites us to draw circles and loops in all directions but the fun increases if you have a round table. We used slippy paint on the DVD. It is a nice feeling and increases speed. We can shoot off snowballs from board and paper or simply draw snowmen.

4. The snow is settling

CD Track 26

Whole body

We lie down on the floor and rest or roll gently from side to side. You could also make slow crawling movements like a polar bear emerging from its den.

On the bo   ard and on paper

As you can see on the DVD we have frothed up the slippy paint on the round table with sponges and the drops that have fallen on the floor are brought together as lying eights. The children make a garland movement on the (table) board which serves as a sledge for Father Christmas. It is a good preparation for the letters r and u.

5. Penguins

CD Track 27

Whole body

We follow each other in a line like penguins with our arms stretched to the music.

This can be done on a roll of wallpaper so that the children remain in a line behind each other.

On the board and on paper

We draw big fish on the wallpaper and the music encourages us to draw little lines for bones and spikes. Next the penguins eat the fish and we encourage the muscles of our mouths by moving the jaws up and down very quickly.

6. Breaking ice

Whole body

Stand whole body and fold your hands.
Stretch and bend your arms in tight angular
movements and turn round slowly. You are
breaking the ice around you.

On the board and on paper

We are sitting on the roll of wallpaper and
drawing large v-shapes around us (over the
fish). Crack! The ice is going to break and you
are going to fall through the ice! We will draw
a row of v-shapes or several variations as Write Drawing has shown you.

7. Ice writing

Whole body

We will be making dancing and skating movements. This music encourages you to dance
just like the Castle Moat music in Dream Castle. While we sit down we allow the arms to
waltz in lying or standing eight positions.

On the board and on paper

The walking eights become a real promenade on a round table. Create this with shaving
cream, paint or chalk. We also waltz on the board and on paper with our eyes closed.

It is snowing!

Snow crystals and stars

Snowstorm

   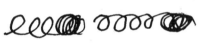

The snow is settling

Penguins

 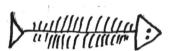

Breaking ice

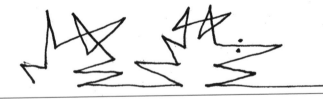

Ice writing